TEACH YOURSELF BOOKS

JAZZ PIANO

Improvisation—that is, the simultaneous creation and execution of musical ideas—is the very essence of jazz piano style. In this book the author outlines for the would-be jazz pianist the musical principles that underlie this form of spontaneous creation. With the help of more than 180 musical examples, he ranges widely over the whole field of jazz piano-playing, showing how the jazz pianist can develop aural perception, discussing the various jazz piano styles that have evolved over the past half-century or so, explaining how jazz rhythms, harmonies and techniques differ from those of orthodox Western music, and examining the relevance of the modal system to jazz. He puts the material over in such a way that the amateur pianist should find that, after a few hours spent with this book, he will already be able to start to create exciting and worthwhile jazz improvisations at the keyboard.

THE AUTHOR

Eddie Harvey is well known on the British jazz scene as a musician, arranger and composer. Closely involved in the post-war revival of traditional jazz in Britain, he then became associated with the 'be-bop' movement, playing with the Club Eleven and the Johnny Dankworth Seven, later the Johnny Dankworth Big Band. During the late 1950s and 1960s he worked with many leading jazz musicians, including Don Rendell, Tubby Hayes and Ronnie Ross, and toured with the Woody Herman Anglo-American Herd and the Maynard Ferguson Band. As an arranger he has been particularly associated with the Humphrey Lyttelton Band and with the Jack Parnell Orchestra at Associated Television. He has lectured on jazz at the City Literary Institute, London, and is at present Assistant Music Master at Haileybury College, Hertfordshire.

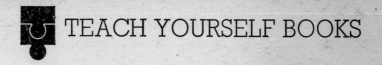
TEACH YOURSELF BOOKS

JAZZ PIANO

Eddie Harvey

ST PAUL'S HOUSE   WARWICK LANE   LONDON EC4P 4AH

First printed 1974

ISBN 0 340 12456 3

Printed and bound in Great Britain for The English Universities Press Ltd by Hazell Watson & Viney Ltd, Aylesbury, Bucks

Contents

	Preface	vii
1	Improvisation	1
2	Rhythm	4
3	Intervals and Relative Pitch	12
4	Harmony (Triads)	20
5	First Steps in Improvisation	25
6	Harmonic Developments	33
7	Early Progressions	41
8	Early Piano Styles	47
9	Further Developments in Harmony	54
10	The Development of the Rhythm Section	59
11	The Diminished Seventh Chord	61
12	Further Dissonance	66
13	Dominant Chords	72
14	The Diminished Fifth Substitution	77
15	The II/V Combination	80
16	Pedal Point	82
17	The Diminished Scale and Its Ramifications	88
18	The Whole Tone Scale	91
19	The Fourth	93
20	Jazz and the Modal System	96
21	The Practical Side	102
22	Some Sequences	111
	Bibliography	162

Preface

As far as I know, nobody has ever learned to play the piano by reading a book on the subject. Nevertheless, I hope that this book will go some way towards helping those who wish to play jazz piano music of their own making. In setting about this task I have attempted to use as little technical jargon as possible, to the extent of simplifying some of the harmonic categorisations in the interest of clarity, for there does seem to be a point at which these systems become so complex that they cease to be useful to the beginner. This is not to say that I have been less than accurate, however, where I have considered it necessary.

I have had to assume some ability on the part of the reader, both as a pianist and as a musician. It is essential to be able to read the examples, for instance, no matter how slowly. Consequently, a little knowledge of the theory of music is required—that is, scales, time and key signatures, note and rest values and so forth. If the reader feels he needs some help in these matters, may I recommend King Palmer's *The Piano* published by Teach Yourself Books; this will provide all the basic groundwork needed for starting *Jazz Piano*.

This book need not be read as a novel, from cover to cover; it is a book for dipping into, and is best read while you are seated at the piano so that you can play and hear the examples. My hope is that its material will act as a spark to exploration: when each chapter is thoroughly understood, the ideas it puts forward should be exploited in as many ways as possible, through keyboard work. This does not mean that the exercises should be simply mathematical constructions. On the contrary, each formula should be turned into music wherever possible, using nuance and accent, light and shade; each formula or device will then become an integral part of your own 'equipment' as a jazz pianist.

Finally, I wish to express my sincere gratitude to Ron Kirkman, H. Clifton Kelynack and Jack Hindmarsh for their help and advice in preparing this book.

E.H.

Acknowledgments

The author and publisher would like to thank the following music publishers for their permission to include certain of their compositions in this book: Southern Music Publishing Co. Ltd. for *Lazy River*, *Rockin' Chair* and *You Can Depend On Me*; Lawrence Wright Music Co. Ltd. for *Ain't Misbehavin'* and *I Can't Believe That You're In Love With Me*; and Campbell Connelly & Co. Ltd. and Belwin-Mills Publishing Corporation for *I'm Getting Sentimental Over You*.

Thanks are also due to Stan Tracy, Harry South, Ken Wheeler, Michael Gibbs, John Warren, Pat Smythe, John Surman and Mike Pyne, all of whom have very kindly contributed to the section on modern jazz compositions in Chapter 22.

1 Improvisation

How do you learn to improvise? By trying to express instrumentally the musical inspiration that comes into your mind, simultaneously with its creation. The basic skill you have to possess in order to do this is that of associating the physical action of playing a note not with a symbol displayed on the written page but with its actual sound. If you read a page of music, this ability is exercised hardly at all. It is therefore essential for you to familiarise yourself as much as possible with the keyboard in terms of sound, both melodically and harmonically. This process helps reading and interpretation; yet how many times do parents tell a child: 'Stop making that noise and play something properly'? Conquering this feeling of guilt is a prerequisite of learning to play jazz: for it is only by experiment that the association between note and sound can be learned. Most jazz musicians seem to have learned their art through this sort of experiment and recommend it as a method. The whole musical memory can be utilised; melodies and harmonies from any source should be attempted without having recourse to the music, as they will all help to train your aural perception.

When commencing this process it is natural to choose melodies and fragments that you prefer, and in this way you begin to acquire a selection/rejection faculty. As you listen to music, you will hear phrases that you like better than other phrases, and it is these that you will attempt to pick out on the keyboard. The importance of spending a great deal of time listening to records, radio, television and live concerts (not only as a critical exercise but also for pleasure) cannot be overemphasised, since so much is absorbed subconsciously. Gradually you will build up a repertoire of phrases; as these are mainly taken from other players and from composers, your playing will be very derivative at first. But this is of little importance at this first stage.

The second stage of development consists of transposing these favourite phrases into other keys. Being able to play them in C alone is not enough, as you will need to play in all keys. The third stage involves linking the phrases together and intermingling them to create other, more original phrases. The final stage consists of creating music that is all your own, using the ability you have acquired from studying other people's music. Do not feel that this is an unethical practice. It is exactly the same method as that used in all forms of art training—students of painting copy old masters, students of harmony and counterpoint study examples of Bach and Beethoven, and so on. One word of warning should be sounded, however: namely, that the process of musical development should be a progressive process. The initial act of studying your own idols should be a help towards evolving a personal means of expression which, provided that an open mind is kept on the subject, will be naturally modified as you live through many years of changing musical experience. A further trap, however, lies in wait for those who become preoccupied with 'style': that if a musician completely alters his preferences with each succeeding fashion he becomes a musical chameleon. Originality springs from having the courage of one's own convictions.

The importance of listening cannot be stressed too greatly. When you are forming your own art style you have to be aware of all the options, and when so many sources of music are available the only limitation is that of time.

There are 'classic' jazz performances that could be looked upon as essential items in a record collection, but, with the never-ending issue, reissue and deletion of records, it becomes difficult to recommend specific albums. However, a list of some of the great names in piano jazz may be useful in this connection. The early blues pianists, such as 'Speckled Red', Romeo Nelson and Jimmy Yancey, are always a joy to listen to, as is the self-styled 'inventor' of jazz, 'Jelly Roll' Morton. The 'rent party' pianists of the 1920s and 1930s (for example, Willie 'The Lion' Smith, James P. Johnson and his pupil in the 'stride' style of piano playing, 'Fats' Waller) are a must in any collection, as is the inventor of 'trumpet-style' piano playing, Earl 'Fatha' Hines. The Chicago-based 'boogie-woogie' school, led by 'Pinetop' Smith, Meade Lux Lewis, Albert Ammons and Pete Johnson, can provide a worthwhile foundation for the beginner, as well as exciting listening. The white pianists playing in Chicago during the late 1920s and early 1930s provided some fine performances: look out for records by Jess Stacy and, later, Joe Bushkin and Gene Shroeder. Four famous band pianists of this era come to mind: Teddy Wilson from the Benny Goodman Trio and Quartet; Billy Kyle from the John Kirby Band; Count Basie, who led his own band; and finally, of course, Duke Ellington, who had so much talent as a composer and bandleader that one tends to lose sight of his prowess at the keyboard. One of the jazz 'greats' is Art Tatum: his all-round mastery, encompassing all the styles of his time (boogie-woogie, stride and blues), allied to his virtuoso technique and a harmonic facility unsurpassed to this day, place him on a special pedestal for many jazz musicians.

The 1940s and the advent of 'be-bop' brought fame to another crop of talented pianists: Thelonius Monk and Bud Powell led the way, and were followed by such men as Dodo

Marmarosa, Al Haig, Duke Jordan and, later, Horace Silver. Other individualists from this fruitful time were John Lewis (who later co-operated with the famous vibraphonist Milt Jackson to form the Modern Jazz Quartet) and that great innovator and teacher, Lennie Tristano. Soon afterwards came Oscar Peterson and Erroll Garner, both masters of the art of piano trio playing.

The 1950s and 1960s witnessed a greater fragmentation of style in jazz than ever before. Possibly the most influential pianist of those years was Bill Evans, who brought to jazz a knowledge of harmony and classical techniques that had not previously been heard. Other fine pianists of this time are McCoy Tyner, Jackie Byard, Roger Kellaway, Mose Allison, Herbie Hancock and men of the late 1960s like Chick Corea and Keith Jarrett. I have no doubt omitted some particular favourites of yours, but I hope nevertheless to have included most of those musicians who have been instrumental in developing the art of piano jazz over the years.

2 Rhythm

The subject of time or rhythm in jazz and its notation has given rise to much confusion over the years. Orchestral musicians often criticise their colleagues in the jazz world for what they rightly consider to be inaccuracies in notation: for there *are* inaccuracies in the notation of jazz, for three main reasons: inadequacies in the system of notation; the subtleties of jazz interpretation; and a basic need for clarity rather than for complication.

The modern system of musical notation is European in origin and was perfected before the advent of jazz. Since jazz developed from an amalgam of European and African music, and since the early jazz musicians were sometimes trained and sometimes not, it is not surprising that subtle differences in rhythmic conception arose which the European system was unable to convey in a simple manner. These differences become strikingly evident when we listen, first, to the recordings of early jazz music and, second, to recordings made in the 1920s by Louis Armstrong. The early musicians, both white (such as the Original Dixieland Jazz Band) and coloured (like Johnny Dodds and Kid Ory) played strictly in $\frac{4}{4}$ time, with what we might call a 'classical' feeling of two notes per pulse, as in either Example 1 or Example 2:

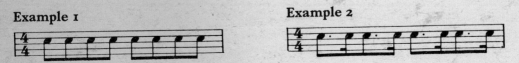

Example 1   Example 2

Thus a typical phrase might sound as in Example 3, with the $\frac{4}{4}$ rhythm closely adhered to:

Example 3

By playing in this way the musicians were possibly harking back to some early tuition and experience in brass or military bands and in playing ragtime, that memorable form of piano music that was so popular at the turn of the century and is currently enjoying a revival.

One of Louis Armstrong's many contributions to jazz, however, was that he became the first musician to 'swing' in the modern sense—that is, in $\frac{12}{8}$ time. This new (to jazz) rhythmic pattern is especially noticeable in his early recordings with the King Oliver Band and in his famous 'Hot Five' and 'Hot Seven' titles with Johnny Dodds and Kid Ory: the contrast between his playing (in $\frac{12}{8}$ time) and that of the other musicians (mostly in $\frac{4}{4}$) is most marked.

Now let us see how this subtle change of basic rhythm affected the notation of jazz. If we assume for the moment that jazz music is played in a time signature that has four main pulses to the bar, the anomaly arises in the subdivision of these pulses. In fact, since the time of the Hot Five and the Hot Seven, most jazz has been played in a true time of $\frac{12}{8}$ divided into four pulses of three quavers. If you beat out a $\frac{12}{8}$ rhythm with the left hand (not too quickly to start with), as shown in Example 4, and then overlay it with a second rhythm

Example 4

Left Hand

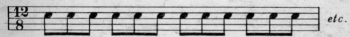

etc.

beaten with the right hand (as in Example 5), then you have the basic jazz rhythm as played

Example 5

Right Hand

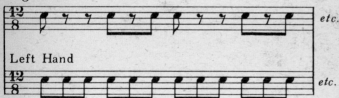

etc.

Left Hand

etc.

by a drummer on his 'top cymbal'. The $\frac{12}{8}$ signature is more obvious at slower tempi, since the faster the tempo the more difficult it is to play the groups of three quavers. We can therefore reduce the rhythm from three to two notes per pulse as follows:

Example 6

etc.

When played with a smoother (legato) method of attack, this rhythm gives us the true 'feel' of modern jazz.

Unfortunately, if we were always to notate jazz in the $\frac{12}{8}$ signature, we should almost certainly find it very complicated to read:

Example 7

For this reason, accuracy seems to have been sacrificed in the interests of simplicity, in that for the purpose of pure notation the $\frac{12}{8}$ signature has been generally replaced by the $\frac{4}{4}$ signature. Thus the phrase in Example 7 would normally be written as in Example 8. The

Example 8

inaccuracy in notation can be seen in greater detail on the first beat of the bar, where the time values of the two notes are

Example 9   **Example 10**

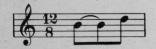   in Example 7 as against

in Example 8. Sometimes one finds the notation simplified still further:

Example 11

It is essential to bear these inaccuracies in mind when reading any music that purports to be jazz. Players who are unaware of it sometimes interpret the notation accurately and, as a result, produce some strange and occasionally hilarious music, in which the melody line may well be jazz-inflected but the rhythm is certainly not.

But since music is an art and not a science, by no means all jazz is played or should be written in $\frac{12}{8}$ time. Ballads, especially, are an exception; and the fact that they are often played in pure common ($\frac{4}{4}$) time does not preclude them from being 'jazz'. Moreover, players of certain forms of jazz have observed quaver notation much more closely, even when playing fast—for instance, the 'boogie-woogie' pianists, the Lennie Tristano school of players, Lee Konitz, Warne Marsh, and so on. Other jazz movements that sprang up on the west coast of America (the so-called 'Cool School') have also adopted a legato 'even quaver' style.

During the last decade or so, jazz has frequently moved away from its basic rhythmic roots. The greater rhythmic complexity that is characteristic of modern music has influenced jazz too, as more and more musicians have come to it after studying in other fields of music. The pianist Dave Brubeck and trumpeter–bandleader Don Ellis have been particularly active in this sphere, utilising time signatures such as $\frac{3}{4}$, $\frac{5}{4}$, $\frac{7}{4}$, and even $\frac{13}{8}$ and $\frac{3\frac{1}{2}}{4}$. The counter-influence of 'pop' music has, on the other hand, tended to promote a return to a true $\frac{4}{4}$ pulse, subdivided normally into quavers and semiquavers; and an $\frac{8}{8}$ rhythm has again become prevalent, for the first time since the days of the 'boogie-woogie' pianists in Chicago. In such cases the mental adjustment from $\frac{4}{4}$ to $\frac{12}{8}$ time is not called for. And now there is a further development—the marrying of these regular time signatures with compound signatures from the modern classical repertoire.

It is thus abundantly clear that jazz, like all music, is in a state of continuous evolution: time signatures that were once a novelty are now commonplace, and the would-be jazz musician should familiarise himself with them as early as possible. First, however, the beginner must become totally familiar with the rhythms in the simpler time signatures and acquire accuracy in their interpretation. He may then move on by adapting the basic signatures into more complex versions so as gradually to extend his experience. (It is worth mentioning here, as a matter of interest, that, compared with wind or string instrumentalists, the pianist is at a disadvantage when learning rhythms, since he has less opportunity for ensemble playing, where problems of rhythmic interpretation can be solved through mutual co-operation.)

Yet merely to count out the main rhythmic pulses is of little use for the purpose of playing jazz. A once-for-all, total assimilation of the basic, familiar rhythms is essential. A good way to achieve this is to tap out the rhythms on two objects giving out different sounds, so that one rhythm may be clearly distinguished from another when they are being played together. The ability to do this is called 'independence'. The basic rhythm should be tapped by one hand or foot and the overlaid rhythm by the other, the purpose being to obtain accuracy in both. By practising Example 5 regularly, for instance, you can improve your rhythmic accuracy for playing jazz, and, as a possible adjunct, a light foot beat on the four pulses in the bar will stabilise it.

When reading the notation in the exercises at the end of the chapter, remember the $\frac{12}{8}$, $\frac{4}{4}$ anomaly mentioned earlier and, if necessary, re-read that section before practising. The exercises should be attempted slowly at first, until accuracy is obtained; then the tempo can gradually be increased.

Exercises

Exercises (*a*) to (*o*) should be played as if they were written in $\frac{12}{8}$ time; exercises (*q*) to (*x*) should be played as printed.

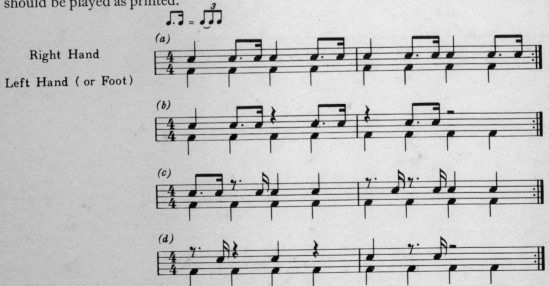

Right Hand

Left Hand (or Foot)

3   Intervals and Relative Pitch

A beginner's first attempts at improvising at the keyboard usually follow the trial-and-error method: he experiments with phrases and sequences, and when he hits upon a happy formula or harmony he commits it to memory. As long as he tackles new material often enough, this exercise is perfectly valid; but as the trial-and-error method can be less interesting to the listener than to the player, it tends to be discouraged. (This could be one of the reasons for the sometimes itinerant life of the budding jazz musician!) An alternative, and more systematic, method of ear training is, however, more beneficial to the student, and at the same time it is more conducive to social and domestic harmony.

Melody and harmony are constructed of tones placed mathematically at varying distances from each other; these distances are called 'intervals'. In the case of melody, the notes are played consecutively; in harmony, they are played simultaneously. In order to play the music we 'hear' in our mind, we must be able to recognise these intervals and thus to choose the correct notes: the ability to do this is called 'relative pitch'. That most easily recognised series of notes, the major scale, serves to illustrate these intervals. Each degree of the scale is given a Roman numeral and a name, as follows:

Example 12

The names of the degrees of the scale indicate their position:

    I   Tonic (key note).
    II   Supertonic (the note above the tonic).
  III Mediant (midway between the tonic and the dominant).
  IV Subdominant (the same distance below the tonic as the dominant is above it).
   V   Dominant (the dominant note of the scale or key).
  VI Submediant (midway between the tonic and the subdominant).
 VII Leading note (the note leading towards the tonic).

If we use the tonic note as the reference point, the intervals between it and the other degrees of the scale are as follows:

Example 13

You will notice that all the intervals are denoted as either 'perfect' or 'major'. However, there are, of course, other notes, namely those in the chromatic scale, and in order to locate the remaining intervals we can either use accidentals (i.e. sharps or flats) or alter the lower reference point to identify them in the diatonic scale. If we first of all use accidentals, we find the remaining intervals as follows:

[handwritten annotations: "minor 2nd 3rd 6th 7th / Diminished 5th / Augmented 2nd 4th 5th 6th" and "Aug 2nd = Mi 3rd / Aug 4th = Dim 5th / Aug 5th = Mi 6th / Aug 6th = Mi 7th"]

Example 14

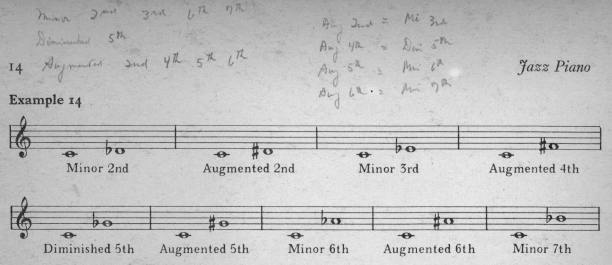

Minor 2nd   Augmented 2nd   Minor 3rd   Augmented 4th

Diminished 5th   Augmented 5th   Minor 6th   Augmented 6th   Minor 7th

Here you will see that an interval that is half a tone below a 'major' interval is called 'minor'; an interval half a tone above a 'major' or 'perfect' interval is called 'augmented'; and an interval half a tone below a 'minor' or a 'perfect' interval is called 'diminished'. Some confusion does admittedly arise in that the diminished interval is a semitone lower than a minor or a tone below a major interval, while it is only a semitone lower than a perfect interval.

In order to recognise these intervals aurally (i.e. without having to find them on a piano), each interval must first be isolated. Taking the major and perfect intervals first, you can sing (either aloud or in your mind) up the major scale from the tonic note until you reach the interval to be practised, whilst at the same time not forgetting the reference note. You can then sing the interval itself. Check the result at the keyboard if one is handy; the exercise itself can be practised anywhere. Thus, by using the tonic note for reference and the major scale, you can train yourself to recognise the major and perfect intervals.

In order to find the 'minor', 'augmented' and 'diminished' intervals, you can either attempt the process as shown in Example 14, i.e. sing up the major scale to the major or perfect interval and then attempt to flatten or sharpen the note to the interval desired, whilst still retaining the pitch of the tonic reference in your mind; or you may find these intervals by using the major scale and altering the reference note.

Example 15

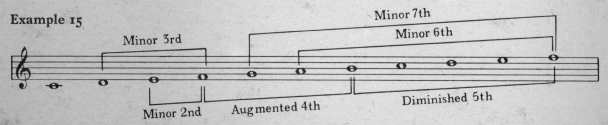

Minor 7th

Minor 6th

Minor 3rd

Minor 2nd   Augmented 4th   Diminished 5th

All three methods should also be practised in reverse: first, by using the tonic note as a reference with the major scale but pitching downwards (Example 16); secondly, by using

Example 16

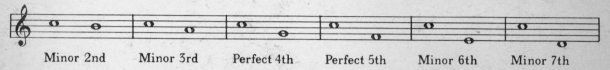

Minor 2nd   Minor 3rd   Perfect 4th   Perfect 5th   Minor 6th   Minor 7th

the tonic note as a reference with accidentals, pitching downwards (Example 17); and,

Example 17

thirdly, by using other scalic reference notes and pitching downwards (Example 18).

Example 18

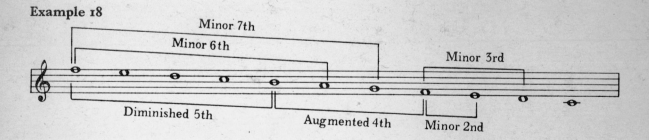

The whole point of the exercise is, of course, to attempt to hear these intervals in as many contexts as possible, until eventually you reach the stage of being able to isolate intervals in which both notes have accidentals, whilst using the tonic note as a reference for both

Example 19

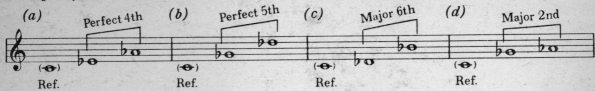

(Example 19). The ultimate aim is to learn to recognise an interval without having any particular reference note to serve as a guide.

Continuous practice, involving the setting up and solving of increasingly difficult problems, is the only way to success in developing your sense of relative pitch. Once you have acquired some ability in recognising 'simple' intervals, i.e. those falling within the compass of one octave, the next step is to tackle 'compound' intervals, i.e. those greater than one octave.

The exercises I have outlined should, of course, be practised in all the major scales, not just in C major as in the examples.

One sure way of making these exercises less academic and more interesting is to attempt to categorise the intervals of familiar melodies. To do this you must first locate the tonic note of the key in which the song is played. The final note of the song is in most cases the tonic note, so you can try to compare the first two or three notes of the melody with the last note by mentally singing through one chorus and starting on a second. Memorise or write down the interval and check your findings at the piano. Since few of us have the gift of perfect pitch (i.e. the ability to name a note upon hearing it, without reference to an instrument), a hypothetical key note may be imagined and the intervals pitched from there.

The categories of intervals

The musical terms 'consonance' (or 'concordance') and 'dissonance' (or 'discordance') are employed to categorise the intervals between notes. Now let us be quite clear about the meaning of these terms from the start, for these are simply technical terms that do not imply any *value* judgments. Many people are under the impression that all concords are pleasant sounds and all discords unpleasant sounds; yet there are many harmonies in the music of Ravel and Debussy, for example, that are utterly agreeable and yet technically dissonant; again, a particular discord may be an offensive noise to one person and an exciting sound to another.

In musical theory, consonances and dissonances are further divided as follows:

The perfect consonances: the octave, unison, fifth and fourth (providing it is not the lowest interval in a chord).

The imperfect consonances: the major and minor third, the major and minor sixth.

The 'soft' dissonances: the minor seventh, the major second, the diminished fifth or augmented fourth.

The 'hard' dissonances: the minor second and major seventh.

The compound forms of these intervals (i.e. the interval plus an octave) also fall into these categories.

By selecting intervals having these particular characteristics, you can construct consonant or dissonant music both melodically and harmonically. It is also possible to use consonant melody with dissonant harmony, and vice versa. The main body of music uses these two factors to manipulate the listener's intellect and emotion, sometimes playing upon one, sometimes upon the other, but generally upon both in varying degrees, most often through alternately creating dissonance and then satisfying the ear by 'resolving' into consonance. Incidentally, the long tradition of resolution into consonance is looked upon by some modern composers as a form of strait-jacket, and they have deliberately turned away from this tradition.

Thickened line

One way to recognise the characteristic sound of each interval is through the use of the so-called 'thickened line'. A single-note melody is sometimes referred to as a 'line'; the 'thickened line' refers to the reinforcement of this 'line' by a second voice or voices moving approximately parallel to it. The supporting voice is usually only approximately parallel to the melody because in diatonic music adjustments have to be made in order to retain the key centre.

Example 20

Completely parallel lines are often used in modern music, however, since the key centre has become of less importance.

Example 21

Exercises should be attempted in which both key-centred and chromatic 'thickened lines' are used.

Exercises

(1) Name the submediant degree of the following scales:

   (*a*) E♭; (*b*) G; (*c*) G♭; (*d*) A.

(2) Name the subdominant degree of the following scales:

   (*a*) D; (*b*) F; (*c*) C; (*d*) A♭.

(3) Construct further exercises on the same principle as Exercises 1 and 2, using the remaining degrees of the scale.

(4) Pitch the following intervals, using the tonic note and the major scale as a reference:

(*a*) major 3rd;   (*b*) perfect 5th;   (*c*) major 7th;   (*d*) perfect 4th.

(5) Pitch the following intervals, using the tonic and the minor scale as a reference:

(*a*) minor 6th;   (*b*) perfect 5th;   (*c*) major 7th;   (*d*) minor 3rd.

(6) Name the notes that are:

(*a*) an augmented 5th from A♭, E, D♭, B and C;
(*b*) a diminished 7th from C, F, B♭, G♭ and A;
(*c*) a diminished 5th from A♭, B, D, G and D♭.

(7) Choose a melodic fragment you know well; after playing it as a single line, convert it into a 'thickened line' regardless of original harmonies, using:

(*a*) 3rds (diatonically);   (*b*) 6ths (diatonically);   (*c*) 4ths (chromatically), etc.

4 Harmony (Triads)

Triads

Having familiarised ourselves with the characteristic sound of each interval, we now progress to the simplest chords. These are named 'triads', because of their three-note construction, and are built up by superimposing two thirds on top of each other. Since there are two types of third (the major and the minor) and two positions for them in each chord, we can combine them in four ways, as follows:

The major chord—minor third over major third.
The minor chord—major third over minor third.
The augmented (5th) chord—major third over major third.
The diminished (5th) chord—minor third over minor third.

Because the intervals differ in the major and minor scales, these triads can be found in various positions in each scale. Let us first consider the major scale. If we construct triads on every degree of the diatonic scale by superimposing one third upon another, we have the following triads:

Example 22

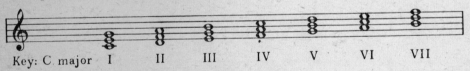

Key: C major   I   II   III   IV   V   VI   VII

You will notice that the type of triad at each interval of the major scale is thus:

Degree	Type of triad
I	major (third)
II	minor (third)
III	minor (third)
IV	major (third)
V	major (third)

VI	minor (third)
VII	diminished (fifth)

On the harmonic minor scale the triads are:

Example 23

Key: C minor   I   II   III   IV   V   VI   VII

Here the type of triad at each interval becomes:

Degree	*Type of triad*
I	minor (third)
II	diminished (fifth)
III	augmented (fifth)
IV	minor (third)
V	major (third)
VI	major (third)
VII	diminished (fifth)

The method of naming triads always creates some confusion, because some triads are called after the characteristic of the lowest third and some after the characteristic of the fifth from the bass note. In the lists above, the interval after which the chord is named has been added in brackets.

We must now go back to the keyboard in order to familiarise ourselves with the characteristic sound of each type of triad and to discover their identities in the various keys.

Triads are categorised as 'primary triads' and 'secondary triads'. The *primary triads* are those that are constructed on the 'tonal' degrees of the major and harmonic minor scales, i.e. those degrees that are primarily responsible for indicating the tonality or key; these are the tonic (I), the subdominant (IV) and the dominant (V). The remaining triads are known as the *secondary triads* and are constructed on the supertonic (II), the mediant (III) and the submediant (VI) degrees of the scales. The supertonic (II) degree of the scale fulfils a function as the dominant note of the dominant degree (as it is a fourth below it) and thus adds a slight reinforcement to the tonality. The mediant (III) and submediant (VI) intervals of the scale do not have a tonal function; they fulfil a very specific role, however, in that they indicate the modality. By flattening or sharpening these two degrees of the scale, we decide whether the scale is to be major or minor. For this reason, they are referred to as the 'modal' degrees. Since there is considerable intermingling of harmony between the major and minor scales based on the same tonic note, they have a most important function, as we shall see later.

Cadences

Cadences are points of rest in music—where the harmony has 'returned to the fold', so to speak. The music process is one of continually placing the listener in a mentally expectant or apprehensive state and then returning him to a state of satisfaction. This may be achieved by moving diatonic or chromatic harmony, which may sometimes involve a complete (though temporary) change of key centre. It is not until the listener returns to the final tonic chord that he finds a complete state of satisfaction; this is the final 'cadence'. However, the journey through a piece of music is not one of continuous travel; there are temporary resting places at intervals that may be compared to the punctuation marks in a sentence, and these are also cadences.

There are four types of cadence: the *perfect cadence*, the *imperfect cadence*, the *plagal cadence* and the *interrupted cadence*. The perfect and imperfect cadences are the equivalent of the full stop and the comma in punctuation, and they use the dominant (V) and the tonic (I) chords of the key:

Example 24

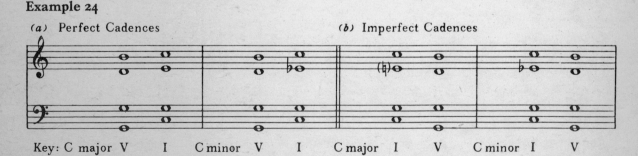

(*a*) Perfect Cadences   (*b*) Imperfect Cadences

Key: C major   V   I   C minor   V   I   C major   I   V   C minor   I   V

The plagal cadence uses the subdominant (IV) and the tonic (I) chords:

Example 25

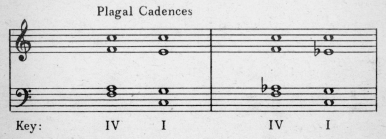

Plagal Cadences

Key: IV   I   IV   I

The interrupted cadence uses the dominant (V) chord, as in a perfect cadence, but instead of going to the tonic (I) chord, as you might expect, it progresses to another, so extending the sequence:

Example 26

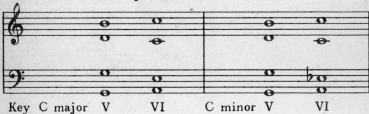

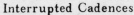

Interrupted Cadences

Key C major V   VI   C minor V   VI

Exercises

(1) Play the major triads based on the following notes:

    (*a*) A; (*b*) D♭; (*c*) B♭; (*d*) E♭; (*e*) F, etc.

(2) Transpose a major triad based on A♭ chromatically (i.e. in semitones) to the same chord an octave higher.

(3) Play the minor triads based on the following notes:

(*a*) D♭; (*b*) F; (*c*) C; (*d*) A♭; (*e*) D; (*f*) B♭, etc.

(4) Play the diminished triads on the following notes:

(*a*) B; (*b*) A♭; (*c*) D; (*d*) F; (*e*) C; (*f*) G♭; (*g*) E♭; (*h*) A; (*i*) E; (*j*) B♭; (*k*) G; (*l*) D♭.

(5) Play the augmented triads on the following notes:

(*a*) C; (*b*) D; (*c*) E; (*d*) F♯; (*e*) G♯; (*f*) A♯; (*g*) D♭; (*h*) E♭; (*i*) F; (*j*) G; (*k*) A; (*l*) B.

(6) Play the perfect cadences (V, I) in the following keys:

(*a*) C; (*b*) A♭; (*c*) F; (*d*) G; (*e*) B♭, etc.

(7) Play the imperfect cadences (I, V) in the following keys:

(*a*) E♭; (*b*) F♯; (*c*) B; (*d*) D, etc.

(8) Play the plagal cadences (IV, I) in the following keys:

(*a*) D♭; (*b*) E; (*c*) F; (*d*) G♭, etc.

(9) Name the primary triads in the following keys:

(*a*) B♭; (*b*) G; (*c*) A; (*d*) E♭, etc.

(10) Name the secondary triads in the following keys:

(*a*) D; (*b*) F; (*c*) G♭; (*d*) D♭.

5   First Steps in Improvisation

Jazz stems from two traditions: first, from the tradition of the vocal music that existed in the southern states of the U.S.A.—the spirituals, the work songs, the blues—and, secondly, from the instrumental tradition of the New Orleans marching bands. Two main jazz styles evolved from these traditions. The vocal music, the structure of which was primarily melody and accompaniment, led to instrumental music of a similar character. On the other hand, the military tradition of the marching bands developed into an improvised contrapuntal music as exemplified by the New Orleans, Dixieland and Chicago styles, and, more recently, by the Gerry Mulligan Quartet, for example. Piano styles were also influenced by these two traditions, as well as by ragtime, which we mentioned earlier.

Many people imagine that the 'blues' is an expression of mood and must always be played at a slow tempo. In fact, the blues is a simple harmonic structure over which jazz musicians can improvise at any tempo, expressing feelings of joy or sadness or any other mood they may fancy. The chief surviving form consists of a sequence twelve bars in length, but there are others of eight and sixteen bars which seem to have fallen from favour at the moment.

The basic sequence may be constructed on either the major or the minor scales and uses primary (I, IV, V) triads only. It is thus an ideal basis for the first steps in improvisation; but before we take these first steps we must look very briefly at the different ways in which the chordal background can be played.

When playing triads we may wish, for one reason or another, to place notes other than the root in the bass. This is known as 'inverting' the chord, and the inversion is indicated by placing a small letter of the alphabet in one of three positions:

(1) The root position, with the root in the bass (Ia).
(2) The first inversion, with the third in the bass (Ib).
(3) The second inversion, with the fifth in the bass (Ic).

If we apply this principle to the tonic (I) chord of C major, we will have the following options:

Example 27

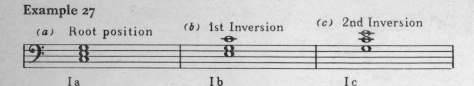

In this book I have as a general rule omitted indications of root position, and chords are in root position unless otherwise indicated.

Now, at last, we can actually sit down at the piano and execute our first improvisations. In our earliest attempts at playing the blues, the melodic line will be carried by the right hand and the accompaniment by the left hand. It is better to start by perfecting the accompaniment first and then adding the improvisation over the top of it. The accompaniment for this first exercise is shown in Example 28.

Example 28

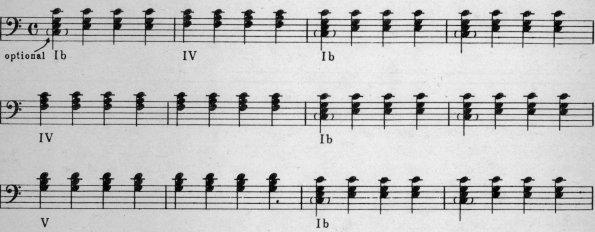

The tonic chord is written in the first inversion (Ib) for ease of execution; the root may be added after some degree of competence has been achieved. Practise the exercise at a slow tempo in the early stages, counting the beats of each bar to ensure accuracy. Once the exercise can be played from memory, a right-hand melody can be superimposed in the treble. This is best added in sections of from two to four bars. Play these bars over and over again, with modifications where needed, until what you are playing corresponds to the melody in your head. Then move on to the next section and carry on practising, frequently playing together the two or more sections you have already worked out, so as to maintain continuity.

You have now reached the start of that creative process where the student himself becomes responsible for the choice of melody. Several common difficulties can arise, however, in the actual execution of the music.

The first problem with which you will probably be faced is that of independence—that is, the simultaneous interpretation of two different rhythms, one to each hand. As we have seen, this skill can be acquired only through constant practice, beginning at a slow tempo and gradually accelerating to the correct tempo as your proficiency grows.

Then there is the question of fingering. Broadly speaking, the best fingering for a phrase is the one that entails the least effort. Some scale work based on the well-known piano exercise books by Beringer, Cramer, Czerny and others will be of great value here. These exercises will strengthen the weaker fingers and help to establish those good hand and finger positions that are so essential for speed, accuracy and tone. (See Bibliography, page 163.)

The third problem is that of your own approach to improvisation. Beginners often fall into two categories: the brave, who will try anything over a given harmony, and the timid, who will often improvise using only chordal tones. I would recommend the former method as being the most fruitful because, whereas you can hardly go wrong when improvising on chordal tones, you have the chance of learning from your mistakes when you are more adventurous. How? In various ways: if you find what you think is a good phrase, you then have to decide whether it fits the harmony; if it *is* a good phrase but does not fit the background, forget the background for the moment, find the most suitable harmony for your phrase and then transpose it into some other keys. Doing this is a good way to help you to remember it.

Another way to benefit from a mistake would be to alter the phrase to fit the harmony (the rhythm of the phrase may, of course, be retained). How do we do this? Briefly, we may state that melody consists of notes that are members of the chords accompanying it and of notes that are not. The former are referred to as 'essential' notes or chordal tones, while the latter are 'unessential' notes or non-chordal tones. Essential and unessential are misleading terms, as are many others in music; they refer to the *harmonic* role of notes only, since obviously all the notes of a phrase are essential to its melodic structure.

Essential notes present no problem, since all you have to do is to check that they are members of the underlying chord. Unessential notes are more complicated, since there are five types:

(1) *Passing notes* occur in rhythmically weak positions and join together the chordal tones in scalic passages (Example 29 (*a*)).

(2) *Auxiliary notes* serve as decorations to chordal tones, moving by step above or below and returning (Example 29 (*b*)).

(3) *Anticipated notes* are chordal tones that appear before their harmony (Example 29 (*c*)).

(4) *Suspensions* are chordal tones that are held into a 'foreign' harmony and then resolved by step (Example 29 (*d*)).

(5) *Appoggiatura* are non-chordal tones that occur on the strong beat and subsequently resolve into a chordal tone by step (Example 29 (*e*)).

Example 29

All these categories of unessential notes may be 'thickened' by the use of one, two or more additional notes.

Example 30

If you categorise the unsatisfactory notes in a phrase, you then know how to alter them and improve the phrase as a result.

Now that we have delved into all these technicalities, a word of warning should be sounded: the creation of a melody is a subconscious act and not one that can be carried out by choosing an essential note here, an appoggiatura there and just a touch of suspension at the end to add piquance, so to speak. Being aware of the various types of notes will eventually affect the subconscious process, however; and then each note, whatever its type, will lie naturally in the phrase, as it should.

The minor form of the blues provides an interesting alternative to the major blues. It can also help us to become more familiar with the minor keys and scales.

The minor blues uses the same degrees of the scale for the bass; but since the minor scale acts as the harmonic source, the triads will have different qualities. The chords constructed on the tonic subdominant and dominant of the harmonic minor scale are therefore as follows:

Example 31

Note that the triads of the tonic and subdominant degrees of the scale are minor triads (the intervals of a minor third superimposed by a major third), while the dominant triad remains the same. Our left-hand accompaniment for the minor blues will then be as follows:

Example 32

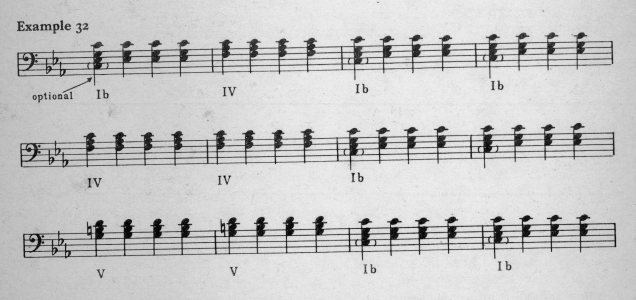

We must now superimpose our improvisation on the accompaniment, this time choosing our melodies from the minor scale.

The student who has listened to recordings of jazz pianists may have noticed that some elements of the minor scale are often used when improvising on the major harmonies. This could be called the 'folk' element in jazz. Instrumentalists sometimes adopt the nuances of vocal blues, that is to say the notes of the flattened third and the minor seventh (E♭ and B♭ in the key of C).

Since this may be your first introduction to improvisation, I have kept the harmonies as simple as possible. This provides us with the maximum number of non-chordal tones, which gives us two opportunities: first, it gives us a clear concept of the harmonies and, as a result, of the key centre; and, secondly, it allows us the maximum melodic freedom. It is one of the paradoxes of music that as harmony becomes more complex it tends to restrict melodic freedom by adopting free-ranging non-chordal tones into the vertical structure. This process began early in the development of music and continues to this day; hence we can observe that harmony is the product of melody, not vice versa as is often thought.

As you will no doubt have noticed, no examples of melodies as such have been included in this chapter. This is an intentional omission since musical composition is a personal art, and one for which the student should take responsibility from the beginning. The exercises are merely *motifs*, which are intended to act as primers rather than as subjects for variation and thus to help the student into an extended improvisation of his own.

Exercises

(1) Improvise on the major blues sequence in Example 28, using mostly diatonic notes and the minor third (E♭) and minor seventh (B♭).

(2) Improvise on the minor blues sequence in Example 32.

(3) Transpose at the keyboard and practise the major blues accompaniment in the following keys, and improvise on them:

(*a*) F;   (*b*) B♭;   (*c*) E♭;   (*d*) A♭;   (*e*) D♭;   (*f*) G;   (*g*) D.

(4) Transpose and practise the minor blues accompaniment in the following keys, and improvise on them:

(*a*) F minor;   (*b*) G minor;   (*c*) D minor;   (*d*) B♭ minor;   (*e*) E minor.

(5) Extend the following melodic fragments into a complete twelve-bar blues:

32

6 Harmonic Developments

Compared to European art music, jazz is a comparative youngster. It has had (and still has) the advantage of being able to draw on the classical tradition when it has felt the need. Basically, however, it remains a folk art and is dependent upon this element for its vitality. Although jazz has on occasion drawn on classical resources, it has also ignored certain aspects of the classical tradition that it may have considered non-essential or restricting. This is not in any way to judge these aspects of musical development as being 'good' or 'bad'; it is simply that they are irrelevant in jazz terms. However, since jazz music evolved at the beginning of the twentieth century (at a time when Debussy, Ravel and Stravinsky were composing in Europe), it was inevitable that it would become more adventurous harmonically, especially after the advent of radio and the gramophone record (the famous piano composition *In A Mist* by Bix Beiderbecke shows how much this is true).

As we have already seen, harmony develops by absorbing notes that have previously been thought of as melodic. Through continual usage these melodic notes become static, being looked upon as vertical combinations with the harmonic background. Thus the primary triads, although still fulfilling the same function in the horizontal development, absorbed the melodic notes and became four-note chords, as did the secondary triads. Jazz at first made little use of the secondary triads—that is, those triads based upon the second, third and sixth degrees of the scale. They did become much more common, however, during the 1930s.

The harmonic major system

Example 33 shows the four-note chords on the degrees of the C major scale. These chords

Example 33

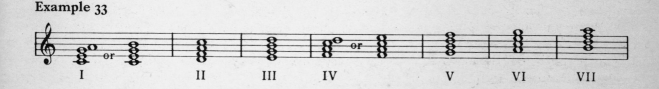

are denoted as follows:

I	C6 or Cma7
II	Dmi7
III	Emi7
IV	F6 or Fma7
V	G7 (the dominant 7th)
VI	Ami7
VII	Bmi7 (5♭) or B half diminished (B∅)

The method of naming four-note chords is unfortunately as confusing as that for the triads. Whilst they take the name of the largest interval, they make certain assumptions about the basic triad which can only be learned by rote. For example, a I chord in the key of C is called a C major seventh (Cma7) after its largest interval, and you are supposed to know that it contains a major triad; and a II chord in the key of C is called D minor seventh (Dmi7) after its largest interval, and here you are supposed to know that it is based on a minor triad. Sometimes, however, the type of triad and the type of largest interval have to be given: for example, a I chord in F minor may have to be called F minor/major seventh (Fmi7♮). The name of the V chord assumes even more: since it is called simply G7, you have to remember that it is a dominant-type chord (V7) that includes a major triad and has as its largest interval a minor seventh.

As in classical music, the first four-note chord to be used extensively in jazz was the dominant seventh (V) chord. This is a most important chord in the major/minor system because it possesses two specific features. First, it is based on the dominant degree of the scale—the degree that most strongly delineates the key by virtue of its physical relationship to the tonic note (in terms of vibrations per second); and, secondly, the chord includes the two 'tendency' tones of the key, i.e. those tones that lead to the tonic chord—the sub-dominant and the leading note. These two notes have a tendency to move in a specific direction: the subdominant to the mediant, and the leading note to the tonic. A simple experiment will demonstrate this: if you establish a key by playing the tonic chord and then play the tendency tone, the direction in which it wishes to resolve will become quite clear.

Example 34

The strong directional pull of the dominant chord is evident throughout harmonic structure, not only in this 'V, I' context but also as a means of returning to the key centre from more remote positions in the system.[1]

In the key system the tonic chord (I) is, of course, equal in importance to the dominant chord, although it plays a more static role. It acts as the final goal, since it has no tendency to move in any other direction. This quality gives it a certain freedom which has been exploited by composers in the 'pop' field. Since it has no tendency to move in a particular direction, it can be moved in *any* direction, needing only melodic reasons to justify it. Many 'pop' tunes have been based on this effect, with tonic chords being moved about by an apparently arbitrary choice. A good example is Jim Webb's *Up, Up and Away*.

The supertonic chord (II) has certain factors in common with both the subdominant and the dominant chord. Its main tendency is to resolve to the dominant chord, since it shares certain notes with the dominant ninth, having a suspended fourth.[2]

Example 35

As with all the minor seventh chords it assumes more importance in modal organisation. The minor seventh chord based on the mediant (III) has factors in common with the tonic chord and sometimes acts as the 'surprise' in an interrupted cadence (V, III).

Since the subdominant (IV) chord in the major can resolve directly to the tonic chord, it often acts as a 'relief' to the tonic: that is, once the tonic has been sounded one can move

[1] See Chapter 7.
[2] See Chapter 15.

to the subdominant, which is then resolved back to the tonic. This cadence, the 'plagal cadence', is often employed in preference to an inordinately long wait on the tonic chord. It is seldom thàt a subdominant chord is used as a 'gateway' into a key in the same way as the dominant. It is sometimes used in conjunction with the tonic minor (I), however, as we shall see later.

In its triadic form the submediant (VI) chord is, in fact, the I chord in the relative minor key. It thus has a special relationship to the tonality. In its four-note 'seventh' form it has much in common with the tonic chord, since it contains the same notation as the third inversion of the tonic sixth chord. It does, however, play a less important role in diatonic major sequences.

The leading note (VII) chord also plays a relatively unimportant role in diatonic sequences, but since it has much in common with the first inversion of the dominant chord it is sometimes used in this way.

All the chords constructed on the major scale have been discussed as elements in diatonic (in key) harmony, but since jazz mostly uses an expanded form of the diatonic system, this involves modulation to other closely related keys. Secondary chords then assume a more important function.

The harmonic minor system

The four-note chords based on the harmonic minor scale are shown in Example 36.

Example 36

Key C minor   I   II   III   IV   V   VI   VII

These chords are denoted as follows:

I	C minor/major 7
II	D minor 7 (5♭)
III	E♭ augmented major 7 (E♭+7♮)

IV   F minor 7
V   G7
VI   A♭ma7
VII   B diminished 7 (B°7)

This list of chords has been constructed merely by superimposing another diatonic third on the triad. In functional terms, several of the chords are seldom found, while certain derivatives of the chords are frequently employed; these often have accidentals that have been 'borrowed' from the major forms.

Example 37

Key C minor   I   II   III   IV   V   VI   VII

The functional chords that are most commonly used in the minor are shown in Example 37 and are denoted as follows:

I   C minor 6 and C minor/major 7
II   D minor 7 (5♭)
III   E♭ augmented 7 (with the minor 7th) (E♭+7)
IV   F minor 6 and F minor/major 7
V   G7
VI   A♭7 (minor 7)
VII   B diminished 7 (B°7)

Before studying the function of each chord based on the minor scale it is worth while comparing them with their equivalent in the major scale (Example 33).

The tonic (I) chord in the minor fulfils a similar function to that in the major, acting as a point of finality since it has no tendency to resolve anywhere. It seems, however, to be less mobile than the tonic major chord, since it does not seem to be so satisfactory to move to a minor key without some kind of preparation (although this could be a personal view).

The supertonic (II) chord in the minor also has a similar role to the II chord in the major, resolving most often to the dominant chord. We might mention in passing that it must also go down in history as the most misnamed chord in the system, since it is invariably confused with the IV6 in the minor—especially in song copies. This could be intentional, of course, since song copies are written for the widest possible consumption and the symbol Dmi7(5♭) could conceivably bring on severe cramp in a novice ukulele player.

The augmented chord based on the third degree of the minor scale is usually used in its first inversion (with the dominant note in the bass). It then becomes an altered dominant seventh chord.

The subdominant (IV) chord in the minor also functions as an alternative to the tonic minor chord in the same way as does the major form (the plagal cadence). It is also frequently 'borrowed' in the major key as it can also resolve the tonic major triad satisfactorily.

The dominant seventh (V) chord in the minor acts in the same way as in the major, since it is identical with the major form. Differences do begin to arise, however, when the ninth is added.[1] The resolution to a final major chord after a predominantly minor sequence ('*Tierce de Picardie*') is seldom heard in serious jazz music.

Since the sixth degree of the minor scale is a modal degree and is flattened in the minor, the characteristics of this chord are totally different from those of a VI chord in the major. It is a major chord in triadic form, whereas the VI chord in the major key is a minor chord. It frequently resolves downwards to the dominant seventh chord. This chord is also borrowed by the major key, in the first inversion, as a 'relief' to the tonic chord (I, VI from the minor, I). It also occurs as a type of imperfect cadence.

Example 38

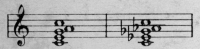

The leading note (VII) chord in the minor is a diminished seventh chord. Since these chords are resolved in so many different ways, I have devoted a whole chapter to them.[2] Suffice it to say that, in this particular context, the diminished chord is often resolved as a first inversion dominant ninth chord to the tonic.

In examining the four-note chords based on all the intervals of the major and minor we have considered them as separate entities. It should, however, be stressed that in practice

[1] See Chapter 12.   [2] See Chapter 11.

the harmonies of the major and minor scales are often intermingled and thus create a single enlarged system based on a common tonic note. The use of key signatures in music tends to give the impression that music is written in a single key, but this is seldom true these days. Often the best one can hope to do when using a key signature is to economise on the writing of accidentals, but in some music it is not considered functional in this role and the music may thus be written in 'open' key (i.e. with no key signature). Most of the modern tunes in the standard jazz repertoire utilise an expanded diatonic system and may call for up to four or five complete modulations in the course of thirty-two bars. This is why it is necessary to transpose any knowledge that you gain in one key into as many other keys as possible.

Exercises

(1) Name and play the four-note chords based on all the degrees of the major scales, starting with G, C, F, B♭, etc.

(2) Name and play the functional chords based on all the degrees of the minor scales, starting with E minor, A minor, D minor, G minor, etc. (see Example 37).

(3) Work out and play with the left hand the following chords, and extemporise over them with the right hand:

    (*a*) G6, C6, F6, B♭6, E♭6, A♭6, D♭6, etc.
    (*b*) Gma7, Cma7, Fma7, B♭ma7, E♭ma7, A♭ma7, D♭ma7, etc.
    (*c*) Emi6, Ami6, Dmi6, Gmi6, Cmi6, Fmi6, B♭mi6, etc.
    (*d*) Emi7♮, Ami7♮, Dmi7♮, Gmi7♮, Cmi7♮, Fmi7♮, B♭mi7♮.
    (*e*) Ami7, Dmi7, Gmi7, Cmi7, Fmi7, B♭mi7, E♭mi7, etc.
    (*f*) Ami7(5♭), Dmi7(5♭), Gmi7(5♭), Cmi7(5♭), Fmi7(5♭), B♭mi7(5♭), E♭mi7(5♭), etc.
    (*g*) A°7, C°7, E♭°7, G♭°7, B♭°7, D♭°7, E°7, G°, B°7, D°7, F°7, A♭°7.

(4) Play the following progression of dominant seventh chords with the left hand, inverting where necessary for easy execution and to ensure smooth horizontal movement, and extemporise over them with the right hand:

    D7, G7, C7, F7, B♭7, E♭7, A♭7, D♭7, etc.

(5) Play the progression II, V, I in the following major keys:

G, C, F, B♭, E♭, A♭, etc.

(6) Play the progression II, V, I in the following minor keys:

E, A, D, G, C, F, etc.

7   Early Progressions

Because the very early forms of jazz were primarily vocal they employed 'singable' intervals, and the harmonic progressions tended to be diatonic, using mostly primary triads. The main interest of this music was, however, melodic, since it was a melody-and-accompaniment form. These melodies had infinite gradations of nuance and accent which it is impossible to notate. We can only be thankful that the gramophone record was invented when and where it was and that some of this early music was preserved as a result, although much fine music has no doubt been lost to us. Since it is impossible accurately to notate the melodic and rhythmic subtleties of this period, I would strongly recommend anyone interested in jazz, no matter what the period or style, to listen to these early performances by artists such as Bessie Smith, Ma Rainey, 'Sleepy' John Estes, Speckled Red, 'Blind Lemon' Jefferson, Bill Broonzy and Lonnie Johnson: they are the very foundation of the music, and remain its prime influence even at the present time. The fact that the technical quality of some of these records was sometimes poor, or the performance 'crude', is of little importance when the music is of such great integrity.

The dominant seventh chord may perhaps have come into jazz from the Methodist hymn tunes of the early settlers or the music of the New Orleans marching bands. Much of the jazz military music these bands played was adapted from the standard marches made popular by composers such as Sousa, and employed the harmony and form of standard military music as it evolved in the nineteenth century. The famous jazz march *High Society* is a typical example.

The dominant seventh was less important as an extra dissonance in the perfect and imperfect cadences than as a chord with strong directional tendencies that encouraged a greater expansion of harmonic resources. In jazz the first such expansion of the system seems to have taken place over diatonic bass movements: for instance, a commonly found bass line is one that progresses back to the tonic through diatonic ascending fourths or descending fifths, as in Example 39.

Example 39

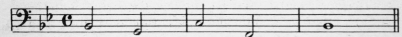

As a purely diatonic chord sequence, this might become:

Example 40

The use of dominant seventh chords could then alter this sequence into the following:

Example 41

Each of these dominant seventh chords is related to the parent key through being the dominant seventh chord of one of the triads in the key. For this reason they are called secondary dominant seventh chords. If you imagine that these triads are I chords temporarily, then, for the purpose of this example, A_7 is the dominant of the II chord (Dmi) in the key of C, D_7 is the dominant of the V chord (G) and G_7 is, of course, the dominant of the key leading to the tonic (I) chord (C). Thus the whole of the sequence would be:

$$\text{I} \quad \text{V}_7 \text{ of II} \quad \text{V}_7 \text{ of V} \quad \text{V}_7 \quad \text{I}$$

An A_7 to Dmi sequence would be shown in Roman numerals as V of II, II; a D_7 to G sequence as V of V, V; and a dominant to tonic sequence as V, I. This is the method of relating secondary keys to the parent key, and it should be thoroughly assimilated as later it will be mentioned frequently.

Since the bass notes remain diatonic while the superstructure becomes chromatic, this creates an expanded diatonic system of harmony.[1] You will also notice that, although a sequence of V chords may be used, they may not necessarily constitute a full modulation (i.e. a change to another key) since a I chord is not used until the end of the sequence, when the parent key has been returned to. Jazz musicians often refer to this continuous progression of dominant chords, by the bass progression of ascending fourths or descending fifths, as 'going round the clock'. This is a reference to the 'key clock' or circle of fifths which shows the relationship of keys to each other and around which a sequence of dominant chords will progress in an anticlockwise direction (Example 42).

Many of the tunes that were popular with the jazz musicians in Chicago in the early 1930s (for instance, *China Boy* and *There'll Be Some Changes Made*) and similar tunes that were composed later (like *Sweet Georgia Brown* and *Lazy River*) were of this type, being constructed of a series of dominant seventh chords resolving one to the other until they reached the tonic chord of the parent key.

When you attempt to play these tunes you will no doubt find that the most common difficulty lies in resolving chords that are ostensibly a fourth up or a fifth down. In fact,

---

[1] This will be discussed at greater length in Chapter 9.

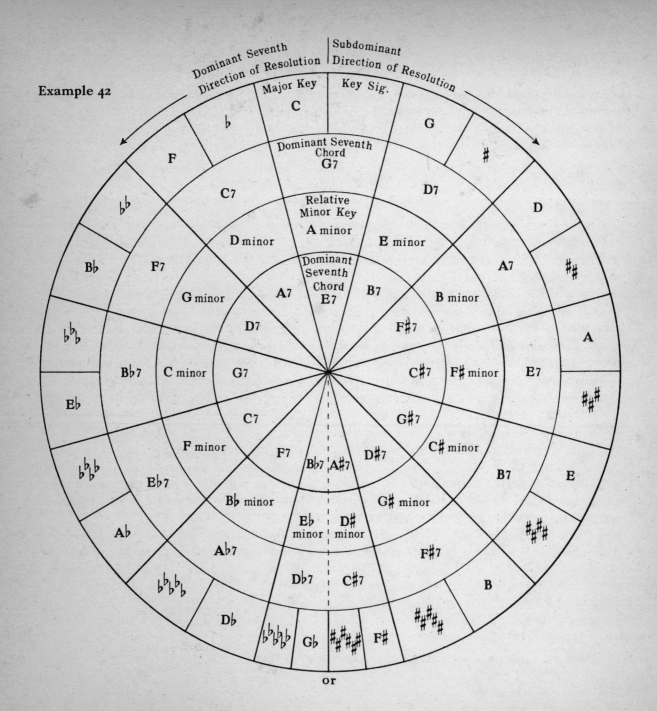

Example 42

successive dominant seventh chords resolve to each other very smoothly if you approach them in the following way: the two internal notes should move downwards chromatically, the seventh dropping to the third of the new chord, while the third drops to the seventh of the new chord, as follows:

Example 43

(a)

If we then add, where convenient, the bass note and fifth (a relatively unimportant component of most root position chords, it seems), we have a smooth transition. In this connection it is not absolutely essential for all chords to be in root position. Once the key centre has been established it is a matter of personal judgment as to which particular inversion of the chord is necessary to maintain the tonality.

(b)

Incidentally, this example shows two ways of 'voicing' chords. When a chord has all its components placed as close to each other as possible, it is said to be in 'close' harmony or voicing. Those chords with an asterisk above them in Example 43 (b) are of this type. The other chords in the exercise are in 'open' voicing: that is, the intervals are wider. A frequent way to introduce an open voicing is to place the second voice from the top down an octave, as in the example. Other spread voicings are called 'open' also if they extend more than an octave.

Exercises

(1) Using the I, VI, II, V, I degrees of the scale as a bass, construct diatonic sequences in the following keys (e.g. in G the sequence would be: G6 or Gma7, Emi7, Ami7, D7, G6 or Gma7):

C, F, B♭, E♭, A♭, D♭, etc.

and extemporise over them.

(2) Using the same bass, construct sequences using a progression of dominant seventh chords in the same keys (e.g. in the key of G major: G6 or Gma7, E7, A7, D7, G6 or Gma7) and extemporise over them.

8 Early Piano Styles

Boogie-woogie

This was an early blues form using a regular left-hand figure or 'ground bass' and played in either $\frac{12}{8}$ or pure $\frac{4}{4}$ time, i.e.

The relatively simple bass figures composed and played by Jimmy Yancey make an ideal first exercise for a student, not only for their ease of execution but also for their appealing charm. Because of the difficulty of capturing their nuance and accent in written notation, the best method of learning this style is by listening to and then copying the figures as Yancey uses them in his recordings. However, a typical example of the simple notation of two of these bass figures is as follows:

Example 44

Once again, it is essential that these bass lines be practised with the left hand only, starting slowly and concentrating on rhythmic accuracy.

The harder, percussive style of boogie-woogie is said to have developed out of the sheer necessity to be heard in the rowdy environments of the mid-west and Chicago saloons. It is again based on the primary chords of the blues form, and once more it is advisable to listen to recorded examples of the style as played by its masters, Pete Johnson, Albert Ammons and Meade Lux Lewis. Lewis' famous *Honky Tonk Train Blues* is an outstanding example of the genre, to the extent of having become a set piece for which the sheet music can now be purchased.

In Example 45 I have given 'models' only of these later bass lines, which must be transposed for the IV and V chord forms and played in the same order as in the example.

Example 45

You will notice that the last of these bass lines incorporates a minor seventh in every chord: this does not necessarily turn these chords into dominant chords since (except for the true V chord) they do not resolve in the usual V, I manner. The minor seventh intervals added to the I and IV chords are once again examples of melody notes being incorporated into harmony. The notes in question, the minor seventh and the minor third of the scale, are the 'folk' elements previously mentioned and are generally known as 'blue' notes. The tradition of adding these notes to the I and IV chords has continued in jazz up to the present time, and in more recent styles, not only of piano playing but also in all jazz. Their existence could also be partly responsible for the adoption of modal organisations by some modern jazz musicians, since these intervals are an integral part of some of these scales.[1]

Stride

The most common error into which students of piano jazz fall seems to be that of attempting too much in the early stages: trying to include *all* the notes in *every* chord in the left hand, to play at a fast tempo and, at the same time, to play a complex right-hand improvisation. This feat becomes particularly difficult when the student tackles the style called 'stride'. This name is derived from the method of accompaniment in which the left hand plays alternately root, chord, fifth, chord in every $\frac{4}{4}$ bar.

[1] See Chapter 20.

Example 46

Before you attempt such a difficult feat you should first familiarise yourself with the harmonies you wish to use by playing block harmonies in minims or semibreves.

Example 47

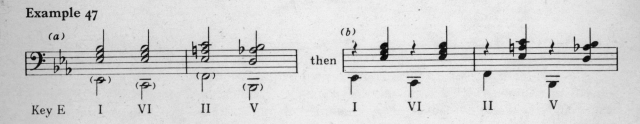

The use of complex harmonies when playing stride left hand is not to be recommended because, first, they are incompatible with the style; secondly, they become difficult to execute; and, thirdly, since the chords sound for such a short period of time they are ineffective. This does not, of course, preclude their use in the right hand.

Once the harmonies have been established it may be advisable to develop some improvisations on them before attempting to animate the rhythm with the 'root, chord, fifth, chord' in the left hand. Solo pianists frequently consider that a stride left hand is essential to maintain rhythmic impetus, but it is important to remember that a melodic line, if it is played rhythmically, is sufficient to maintain movement. At the points of rest in such a line a rhythmic counter-melody may also be used to offset any loss of impetus. If you listen to even the great exponents of stride, you will notice how often they relieve the left-hand rhythm with breaks, often saving the stride rhythm for rhythmic climaxes. Although he was not noted as a stride pianist (or even as a jazz pianist in the view of some 'authorities'), Art Tatum demonstrates one of the most tasteful uses of the style, alternating it with 'walking' tenths and rubato sections to create music of great variety and interest. It is most important when playing stride piano to ensure rhythmic accuracy, and this can best be achieved by playing lightly with a bouncy feel rather than with the heavy 'thrashing' one hears so often.

A variation of the stride style of piano playing, usually played at a medium or slow tempo, is the 'vamp'. In this style, which has long been favoured by light music or 'dance' pianists, a tenth is alternated with a chord in closed position. These tenths are usually 'flipped', and the style is sometimes played with the root followed by the tenth and sometimes vice versa.

Example 48

If one has a hand of average size, the physical difficulties of playing tenths are great: hence the necessity to 'flip' the interval. In order to hear the interval as a whole, considerable use has to be made of the sustaining pedal, which tends to 'blur' the harmony and imparts an over-rich quality to the texture. For this reason my own preference is to avoid the method, but this is purely a matter of personal taste. This is not to deride the tenth, provided that it is used with discretion and it is physically possible to play the two notes together.

The 'walking' tenth has been most effectively played by Fats Waller, by Art Tatum and by the man most usually associated with it, Teddy Wilson. It is almost impossible to state any rules regarding the 'walking' tenth, since it involves so much chromatic movement. The tenths may 'walk' to a point of resolution both diatonically and chromatically, and once more the best way to become familiar with this piano style is to hear it on a recording by one of the three pianists mentioned. Example 49, which is a blues, attempts to give some idea of the technique.

Example 49

Exercises

(1) Practise the slow boogie left-hand figure in Example 44 and extemporise over it.
(2) Transpose and play in other keys.
(3) Construct a twelve-bar blues from a figure in Example 45 and extemporise over it.
(4) Practise a stride left hand using root, chord, fifth, chord on the following short sequences and extemporise over it:

(b)

3 times					
‖: F ⁄ Dmi ⁄	Gmi7 ⁄ C7 ⁄ :‖ F ⁄ ⁄ ⁄	F ⁄ ⁄ ⁄ ‖

Key F	I	IV	II	V	I	I

(c)

3 times					
‖: G ⁄ E7 ⁄	Ami7 ⁄ D7 ⁄ :‖ G ⁄ ⁄ ⁄	G ⁄ ⁄ ⁄ ‖

Key G	I	V of II	II	V	I	I

(d)

3 times					
‖: B♭ ⁄ B♭7 ⁄	E♭ ⁄ E♭mi ⁄ :‖ B♭ ⁄ ⁄ ⁄	B♭ ⁄ ⁄ ⁄ ‖

Key B♭	I	V of IV	IV	IV	I	I

(5) Construct a left-hand pattern using the stride style based on a twelve-bar blues and extemporise over it.

(6) Construct a left-hand pattern using the 'vamp' style based on a twelve-bar blues.

(7) Starting with an interval of a major tenth, based on C, try 'walking' it up the keyboard (in regular tempo) using black notes occasionally to place diatonic harmonies on a strong beat (this exercise is purely experimental).

(8) Experiment by 'walking' the tenth downwards.

9   Further Developments in Harmony

Secondary dominant chords in the major

In Chapter 4 we discussed the structure of the triads based on the degrees of the major scale (Example 22) and we saw that the triads on the degrees from I to VI were either major or minor. If we once again consider these chords as tonic (I) chords in their own tonalities, we shall notice that they belong to two major keys and their relative minors. In the case of the key of C, the tonic chord is obviously in its own key, as is the chord of the relative minor, which is based on the VI degree. The subdominant (IV) chord could be a tonic chord in the key of one flat (F), as could the chord based on the supertonic (II) degree, D minor, which is the relative minor key of F. The dominant (V) triad is the tonic chord of the key of one sharp (G), and the remaining degree, the mediant (III), is its relative minor triad. The leading tone triad is diminished and thus cannot be considered as a I chord in any tonality.

Example 50

Because these three keys, C, F and G, are linked in this way, they work in conjunction with each other and form an expanded diatonic system. It will be noticed, incidentally, that the three keys are neighbours in the 'circle of fifths' (Example 42), the parent key being in the middle. The expanded diatonic system utilises not only those chords that are common to the tonalities but also the supertonic (II) and dominant (V) chords of those tonalities. Let us now construct a series of short harmonic 'sentences' so that we can play, and thus hear, this relationship. What criteria should we adopt for their construction? First, it is essential to begin and end in the parent key. Secondly, we must modulate to the secondary key, and we must therefore use the tonic chords of both keys. The most effective way to modulate into the tonalities is, of course, through the dominant seventh (V7) chord, because of its special qualities (tendency tones, etc.), which we have already discussed. We shall now carry out this exercise on each degree of the scale from II to VI, as follows:

Example 51

(a)   I,   V7 of II,   II,   V7,   I.

(b)   I,   V7 of III,   III,   V7,   I.

(c)   I,   V7 of IV,   IV,   V7,   I.

(d)   I,   V7 of V,   V,   V7,   I.

(e)   I,   V7 of VI,   VI,   V7,   I.

If we express these numerals in terms of chord symbols in the key of C, they will look as follows:

Example 52

(a)   C,   A7,   Dmi,   G7,   C.

(b)   C,   B7,   Emi,   G7,   C.

(c)   C,   C7,   F,   G7,   C.

(d)   C,   D7,   G,   G7,   C.

(e)   C,   E7,   Ami,   G7,   C.

These 'sentences' are frequently extended by delaying the resolution to the parent key, sometimes to the extent of turning them into a 'round-the-clock' series of dominant chords (the common device that we have already mentioned). Let us consider each sequence in turn, omitting the tonic chord since this does not modulate.

The sequence on the II chord has been utilised as a basis for many tunes. With the chromatic alteration to Dmi (thus converting it into D7) it is found in *Ja-Da, Hurry On Down To My House, Baby* and the well-known Sonny Rollins tune *Doxy*, for instance.

The second sequence (on the III chord) appears in the tune *The Best Thing For You Would Be Me* from *Call Me Madam*, starting on the V of III and omitting the first chord (I).

The IV sequence is found in *'Deed I Do* and in the twelve-bar blues generally, where it is extended by the intrusion of the tonic chord (shown in brackets), as follows:

Example 53

I, I, I, V of IV, IV, IV, [I, I], V7, V7, I, I.

in the fifth bar of *I Got Rhythm*, where it is extended by the IV chord from the minor and the tonic chord:

Example 54

I   VI, II, V7, I, VI, II, V7, I, V7 of IV, [IV   ], I, V7, I.
from C minor

in the first two bars of the middle eight bars of *Honeysuckle Rose*, and in innumerable other sequences.

The V sequence occurs in *Exactly Like You, Big Butter and Egg Man* and, starting on the V of V, in *I Cover the Waterfront, Tangerine* and *I Got a Right to Sing the Blues*.

Finally, the sequence for the VI chord has been used in chromatically altered and extended form for *Basin Street Blues, Who's Sorry Now?, All Of Me* and *As Long As I Live*. Since music is an art and not a science, where melody is sometimes the product of harmony and harmony is the servant of melody, few of these sequences are used as a basis for standard tunes *in toto*. Nevertheless, it can clearly be seen how these relationships have inspired the basic idea behind many compositions.

Secondary dominant chords based on the harmonic minor scale

When attempting this same process in the minor keys, we find that there are fewer opportunities to create 'sentences', since the triads on the second and third degrees are neither major nor minor and cannot therefore act as temporary tonic chords. Moreover, the leading note triad (since it still has the diminished quality it had in the major) still cannot represent a tonality. This leaves us with the I, IV, V and VI degrees of the scale as a basis for experiment.

Example 55

Secondary Key signatures

I	II	III	IV	V	VI	VII
Minor	Diminished	Augmented	Minor	Major	Major	Diminished

Once again we need not consider the tonic chord, since it does not modulate.

If we use the same criteria as we did in the major, the sequences will appear as follows:

Example 56

(*a*) I, V7 of IV, IV, V7, I.

(*b*) I, V7 of V, V, V7, I.

(*c*) I, V7 of VI, VI, V7, I.

We can express these Roman numerals in terms of chord symbols as follows:

Example 57

(*a*) Cmi, C7, Fmi, G7, Cmi.

(*b*) Cmi, D7, G, G7, Cmi.

(*c*) Cmi, Eb7, Ab, G7, Cmi.

The V of IV sequence is used in Johnny Carisi's beautiful minor blues *Israel*, and in *Lullaby of the Leaves*. The V of V sequence occurs in *Love Me Or Leave Me* and *Lullaby of Birdland*, and the more recent tune *Sunny* utilises the V of VI sequence. A further sequence can be taken from the melodic form of the minor scale, which in the descending form uses a lowered leading tone (Bb in Cmi), thus forming a major triad on the minor seventh degree. This is the basis of a 'pop' song from France called *Love Is Blue*.

It must be stressed again how important it is that you should become familiar with these sequences in all keys, since most tunes consist of a series of modulations that may commence in the parent key, move to a secondary key and then slowly return to the tonic of the parent key after passing through other keys. Other tunes may commence in a foreign key and reach the parent key only after a series of modulations at the very end. The beautiful 'standard' *Laura* is a classic example of this kind of structure.

Exercises

(1) Transpose Examples 51 and 52 into *all* keys. This is an important exercise which should, if necessary, be written out first and then played. Extemporise over.

(2) Transpose Examples 56 and 57 into *all* keys and extemporise over.

10 The Development of the Rhythm Section

The various piano styles discussed in Chapter 8 were developed by solo pianists and remained unchanged even when the pianists played in rhythm sections (that is, string bass or tuba, drums and sometimes guitar or banjo). This state of affairs continued until the rise in popularity of Count Basie's orchestra in the mid-1930s, when Basie's famous rhythm section, then composed of Jo Jones on drums, Walter Page on bass and Freddie Green on guitar, engendered a new conception of swinging rhythm. This new conception enabled the Basie band to develop a more economical style of playing which imparted a lighter texture to the music and provided a more subtle backing for its great soloists: Lester Young and Herschel Evans on tenor saxophones, Buck Clayton on trumpet, and Dicky Wells and Vic Dickenson on trombones. Basie's own piano solos had previously been in the stride style; now, however, they underwent a change, allowing the rhythmic function to be taken over completely by the bass, drums and guitar, with Freddie Green, the guitarist (who was primarily responsible for the new rhythmic conception), also being responsible for much of the harmony. His solos thus became mostly single-line right-hand improvisations, with chordal punctuations in the left hand. This style influenced other pianists and led to a new and more subtle approach to rhythm generally, with the earlier 'on the beat' statement of the rhythm being replaced by a syncopated style that implied rather than stated the rhythm. This new approach laid the foundations for the further changes that occurred in the early 1940s under the general name of 'be-bop'.

The unfortunate title 'be-bop', which was thought up by a New York disc jockey as a kind of sales gimmick, nevertheless did indicate accurately the percussive, fragmented texture of the new music. At that time there seems to have been a general desire to escape from an over-apparent statement of rhythm in favour of a more subtle approach. Building on the foundations already laid by Count Basie and his rhythm section, players developed new rhythmic ideas, and this in turn led to a breakthrough in techniques. In some ways it is ironic that one of the first of the new developments was a fall in the popularity of the guitar as a rhythm instrument, since Freddie Green had played as big a part as anyone in the breakthrough.

This new freedom gave the pianist greater scope, since he was no longer obliged to conform to such a rigid harmonic structure, nor to state the basic pulse. It also gave rise to a new breed of virtuoso bass players under the influence of men like Jimmy Blanton and, later, Oscar Pettiford, both of whom worked with Duke Ellington's band. These players no longer confined themselves to the traditional bass role of playing mostly roots and fifths but instead played 'walking' lines of notes. The final characteristic of the new freedom in jazz developed under the influence of Kenny Clarke, who emancipated drummers from their purely time-keeping role and fostered a greater independence of rhythm between the two hands, since from now on one hand only marked out the time whilst the other filled in with decorations. This created a pattern rather than a simple metronomic beat.

But rhythm was not the only area of change during this fruitful period. The two giants of the be-bop era, Charlie Parker the alto saxophonist and Dizzy Gillespie the trumpeter, had perfected a more chromatic approach to jazz harmony, under the influence of men like pianist Thelonius Monk, the *éminence grise* of the movement. The be-boppers also formulated a more oblique form of improvisation than that favoured by the previous generation of jazz giants such as Louis Armstrong, Roy Eldridge, Lester Young and Coleman Hawkins. Their improvisations were less trammelled by bar lines than were those of their predecessors, and they utilised intervals and harmonies that were more chromatic and dissonant.

The influence of these new trends on jazz pianists was considerable. The first effect was that pianists came to prefer working with rhythm sections and concentrated less on becoming solo performers. Although this was a loss in one direction, as there has always been a great tradition of solo pianists in jazz, it nevertheless allowed pianists the freedom to explore new facets of music, since they were no longer restricted to the old time-keeping role. Abandoning this role also meant that pianists could develop a right-hand solo technique. This may seem to pose a problem for the student, who may think that he must deliberately choose between two styles of playing. This is a decision that need not be taken consciously, however. The natural selection of the kind of music you wish to play will dictate the style to be adopted.

11 The Diminished Seventh Chord

The diminished seventh chord, which appears on the VII degree of harmonic minor scale (see Example 37), is so called because its largest interval is a diminished seventh (i.e. one semitone lower than a minor seventh or, enharmonically speaking, a major sixth); but in addition it possesses other characteristics that make it unique. Its triad consists of two minor thirds, one above the other, the higher interval forming a dissonant tritone (diminished fifth) with the bass note:

Example 58

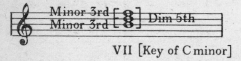

VII [Key of C minor]

A further minor third is superimposed on the triad to form a diminished seventh with the bass note:

Example 59

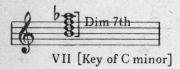

VII [Key of C minor]

This creates a chord composed of two interlocked tritones, a dissonant interval which has a tendency to move to a consonant interval. One might imagine that this chord would be strongly tonal as a result. The converse is true, however: when standing alone, diminished seventh chords have a particularly atonal quality. Another unique characteristic of the diminished chord is its symmetrical structure, since all its voices are equidistant from each other (minor third). Consequently its inversion forms are very similar in sound, which makes it difficult to identify the true bass note and hence to name the specific chord (since a chord takes its name from its bass note). A further result of this symmetrical structure is that the diminished seventh chord, when moved up or down chromatically, reaches an inversion of itself after moving a minor third: thus, for the sake of convenience, one could state that there are only three diminished seventh chords, plus their inversions.

Example 60

Because of its ambiguous tonality and its strong tendency to move, the diminished seventh chord resolves satisfactorily in a number of ways.

The first resolution may be called the 'regular' one, since it stems from the chord's relationship with the dominant minor ninth chord (V9♭), again taken from the minor scale. If you think of the diminished seventh chord as being synonymous with the first inversion of the dominant minor ninth (i.e. with the third in the bass), it will resolve as the dominant chord would (i.e. V, I). An alternative way to look upon this kind of resolution is to imagine the chord as it appears in the minor scale (i.e. on the VII degree or leading tone), in which case the chord resolves, as its name implies, to the tonic chord (VII, I major or minor) through the root ascending by a semitone.

Example 61

Both these ways of remembering the movement are valid, since they both dictate that the passing notes in a phrase played over the sequence will be drawn from the appropriate harmonic minor scale, or major scale with the sixth flattened. This kind of resolution is often found when the diminished seventh chord is used as a link between the I and II, and the II and III chords of the major.

Example 62

Both are utilised by jazz musicians in the opening bars of *Ain't Misbehavin'*.

A variation on this kind of resolution of the diminished seventh is used to link the tonic chord with the dominant seventh in its second inversion, as a result of voice movement.

In the regular resolution of the diminished seventh, the bass parts ascend in order to resolve. They may also fall, particularly between the first inversion of the tonic chord and supertonic chord (II). This is sometimes used in *Talk of the Town*:

Example 63

A similar type of movement occurs between the second inversion of the tonic chord and the subdominant chord:

Example 64

This sequence is often reversed, with an ascending bass line being used (Example 65).

Finally, the diminished seventh chord is sometimes used as a kind of relief chord to the tonic chord, by two voices falling a semitone and then returning (auxiliary notes).

Example 65

Key F   IV [Dim 7 link]   Ic   V of II

When dealing with diminished seventh chords it is important to categorise which type of resolution is being used, since the name of the chord will depend upon the bass movement and will indicate the choice of passing notes. As a general comment, we should state here that these resolutions are not 'rules' as such; they are just common ways of using the diminished seventh chord. Further uses are discussed in Chapter 17.

Exercises

(1) Play the chord of C^o7 and move it upwards chromatically until it reaches its next inversion.

(2) Play C^o7 and move downwards chromatically until it reaches its inversion.

(3) Study Example 61 and transpose it into major and minor keys, starting with G, C, F, B♭, E♭, D♭, etc.; extemporise over.

(4) Study Example 62 and transpose it into all keys.

(5) Study Example 63 and transpose it into all keys.

(6) Study Example 64 and transpose it into all keys.

(7) Study Example 65 and transpose it into all keys.

12 Further Dissonance

In the introduction to Chapter 6 we saw how jazz musicians have drawn on the resources of classical music as and when they felt the need, developing jazz in their own way by selecting from and utilising classical techniques as they thought best. In the modern musical world, dissonance has reached such a stage of development that any combination of vertical tones may be justified by a composer, be he in jazz or of the European classical tradition. This presents a problem for the author of any book on harmony, since at a certain stage he inevitably begins to select his personal preferences from the vast number of options available. To do so here would be to contradict the aim of this book, which is to help the reader to create his own music. It is therefore necessary to define our terms of reference as we reach this stage.

This chapter discusses vertical combinations of notes up to the stage where it can be said there is still a standard, common practice among musicians who play jazz. *Avant-garde* developments in jazz do not conform to this standard, and quite rightly so: for how could new developments take place otherwise? It should thus be repeated that, as well as and beyond the methods discussed in this book, the arbitrary choice of the individual himself must also be taken into account; or, to use the current jargon, 'do your own thing'. If it sounds right to you, then it is right. Most free-thinking musicians seem concerned that they should develop in both directions, believing that each complements the other.

Having made these general points, let us now continue our investigation into further dissonance by superimposing yet another row of thirds over the seventh chords we met in Chapter 6, thus creating a series of ninth chords, firstly in the major key:

Example 66

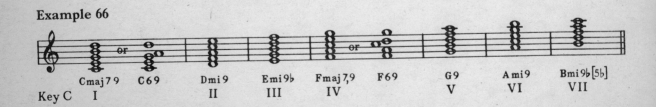

You will notice that some of the ninths seem to create a more satisfactory harmony than others, although these notes may, of course, be treated as accented passing notes and resolved into other harmonies by moving them by step. The ninth chords based on the mediant and leading note degrees of the scale fall into this category, in my view. The minor key also creates a number of unsatisfactory ninths which are seldom used in their pure form.

Example 67

Key C minor

| Cmi7♮,9 | Cmi6 9 | Dmi9♭[5♭] | E♭+7♮,9 | Fmi9 | G 9♭ | A♭7♮,9♯ | D°7,9♭ |
| I | | II | III | IV | V | VI | VII |

Notice how the modal degree of the VI changes not only the supertonic triad in the major and minor but also the dominant ninth chord in the two modalities (G9 to G9♭).

In practice, some altered forms of the ninth chords based on the minor scales are more frequently found. Some of the intervals are taken from the melodic minor scale:

Example 68

| Cmi7♮,9 | Cmi6 9 | Dmi9 [5♭] | E♭+9 | Fm7♮,9 | G 9♭ | G9♯ | A♭9 | Bmi9[5♭] |
| I | | II | III | IV | V | | VI | VII |

These are extensions of the chords found in Example 37.

You will notice that if you continue to superimpose diatonic third intervals above a root, the sequence repeats itself after two octaves (i.e. at the fifteenth):

Example 69

I mention this here as an encouragement for you to stay with this practice, as we only have two more intervals to add: the eleventh and the thirteenth.

The chords of the eleventh are as follows:

Example 70

Key C   I   II   III   IV   V   VI   VII

Once again, we have some unsatisfactory dissonances which may be resolved, as explained previously, as appoggiatura or passing notes. The chromatically altered eleventh chords more frequently found in jazz are as follows:

Example 71

Key C   I   III   IV   V   VII

The introduction of an augmented eleventh interval may seem to be incongruous, but this interval is not such a stranger as it at first appears: it belongs to the harmonic series of notes, based on the root, being the eleventh partial.

The more common eleventh chords in the minor are as follows:

Example 72

I   II   III   IV   V   VI   VII

The final interval may now be added, the more frequently found thirteenths being in the major:

Example 73

I   II   III   IV   V   VI   VII

and in the minor:

Example 74

II   IV   V   VI   VII

A comprehensive chart of all these extensions (in the key of C only) may now be constructed:

Example 75

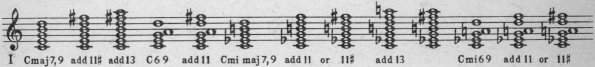

I   Cmaj7,9   add 11♯   add 13   C6 9   add 11   Cmi maj7,9   add 11   or   11♯   add 13   Cmi6 9   add 11   or   11♯

II   Dmi9   add 11   add 13   Dmi7, 5♭, 9   add 11   add 13

III   Emi9   add 11   add 13   E♭+ maj7, 9   add 11   E♭+9   add 11♯

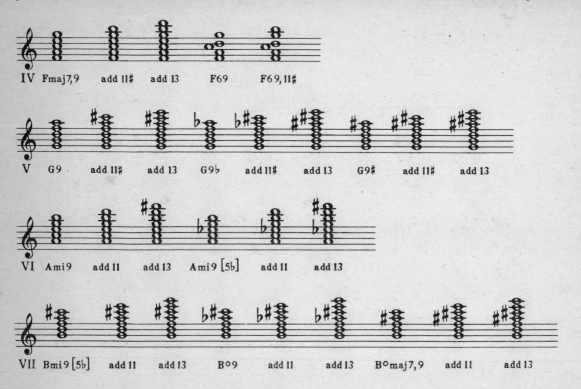

As a word of encouragement, I should add that few of these chords are used *in toto* because of the pianistic difficulties of playing simultaneously chords that contain five or more notes— but one must remember that a line of melody may *imply* harmony by its very choice of notes. Notes played consecutively can be just as effective in portraying harmony, since the mind remembers them for a period, however brief. Furthermore, the method of building vertical dissonances by superimposing thirds should be regarded merely as a method of finding out what harmonies are available. It is by no means the only way of arranging notes, and indeed other distributions of the same notes may be both more effective and easier to play; for instance :

Example 76

Cmi6 9   Ebmaj 7

In conclusion, we may state that all the elements of five- or six-part chords may not necessarily be essential for producing their characteristic sound. Having constructed a full chord by the 'building thirds' method, we should investigate its properties *as a sound* by playing it at the keyboard and then experiment by leaving out some of the elements and seeing whether they are essential to the basic character of the harmony.[1] The third plus one or two of the characteristic notes is sometimes found to be sufficient for this purpose. As always, however, personal experiment is the most successful way of finding out what is adequate and what is not.

Example 77

F 13   C9   Eb 69

Exercises

(1) Transpose Example 66 into all keys, starting with G, C, F, Bb, Eb, Ab, Db, etc.
(2) Transpose Example 68 into all keys, starting with Emi, Ami, Dmi, Gmi, Cmi, Fmi, Bbmi, etc.
(3) Transpose Example 71 into keys G, C, F, Bb, Eb, Ab, Db, etc.
(4) Transpose Example 72 into keys Emi, Ami, Dmi, Gmi, Cmi, Fmi, Bbmi, etc.
(5) Transpose Example 73 into keys G, C, F, Bb, Eb, Ab, Db, etc.
(6) Transpose Example 74 into keys Emi, Ami, Dmi, Gmi, Cmi, Fmi, Bbmi, etc.

[1] See Chapter 21.

13   Dominant Chords

No doubt the chart of chords in the previous chapter (Example 75), and the prospect of transposing them into all twenty-four keys, will have produced a trauma in even the keenest reader, which hoary platitudes such as 'Rome wasn't built in a day' will do very little to dispel. While the more academically minded may set about learning the transpositions methodically, others may take comfort from the fact that, after an initial period of practice, the sound of a particular combination or formula will become established in the mind, and you will find yourself trying to apply this sound to your own music almost subconsciously. This often succeeds in ruining the music temporarily, because you will tend to introduce it in every possible situation; but the device will eventually take its place in your harmonic stock, so to speak, to be used when the time seems appropriate. The over-exposure is necessary, however, in order that the harmony may be firmly fixed in your memory in the first place.

This over-exposure happens particularly with the dominant chord, because it occurs so frequently. Fortunately we have a wide variety of such chords at our disposal, as can be seen from the chart (Example 75). One variety we have not mentioned so far, however, is the dominant seventh chord having a diminished fifth (which may also be looked upon as an augmented eleventh). The triad is seldom used in jazz.

Example 78

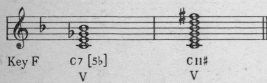

As we saw in Chapter 12, the augmented eleventh has a closer relationship to the root than is at first apparent. If we add this chord to the chart in Example 75, we may notice that the characteristic intervals on dominant chords fall into two areas which I call the 'variable areas', for reasons that will become clear. There are two such areas, each containing four notes. In addition, we must have the essential notes of the dominant seventh chord: the root and the two tendency tones, the third and the seventh. We may choose any two 'characteristic' notes, one from each variable area.

Example 79

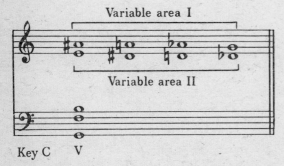

Key C   V

By permutating the four notes in the one area with the four notes in the other area, we have an easy way of memorising sixteen types of dominant chord.

Example 80

(a)

G 13 [9#]   G 13   G 13 [9♭]   G 7 [13]

(b)

G+9#   G+9   G+9♭   G+7

Key C   V   V

Another benefit that derives from a knowledge of these variable notes is that, if you wish to vary the harmony around a single note, you may move the chord around the note.

Example 81

Yet another use can be made of this 'area' thinking: if a melody falls to a long note over a dominant chord, we may continue the rhythmic interest by using a counter-melody situated in the other area from that in which the long note lies.

Example 82

Finally, the situation sometimes arises where it is necessary to have a tonic note over dominant harmony. This can be attained in an obvious manner, yet it is surprising how often it puzzles students. You simply omit the leading tone, and thus obtain the following solution:

Example 83

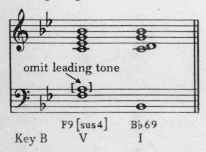

F9 [sus4]   Bb69
Key B   V   I

No doubt all the alternatives will seem complicated from the point of view of their notation. However, one method of simplification that seems to be popular among jazz players is the use of 'false' categorisations incorporating characteristic notes: for instance, the dominant chord C13(11$\sharp$) may be thought of as $\dfrac{\text{D}}{\text{C7}}$.

Example 84

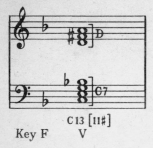

C13 [11$\sharp$]
Key F   V

Here are some more cases where false categorisations may be used (this method is useful for discovering unusual arpeggi also):

Example 85

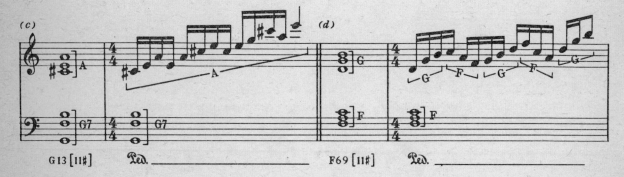

Exercises

(1) Work out the variable areas on the following dominant seventh chords by choosing one note from each area and combining it with the root, third and seventh of the chord:

D7, G7, C7, F7, B♭7, E♭7, A♭7, D♭7, etc.

(2) Choose a note in one area and move the dominant chord around it chromatically.

(3) Choose a note in the other area and move the same chord around it chromatically.

(4) Play a tune that contains an imperfect cadence and play a counter-melody in the opposite area to that in which the melody lies.

(5) Play Example 83 and transpose into all other keys.

(6) Play Example 85 (*a*) and (*b*) and transpose into all other keys.

14 The Diminished Fifth Substitution

Having familiarised ourselves with the dominant augmented eleventh or diminished fifth chord, let us now compare two dominant chords of this type taken from two different keys—Gb and C—the root notes of which are a diminished fifth apart:

Example 86

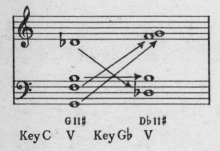

Key C   V   Key Gb   V

You will notice that these two dominant chords possess identical notes, harmonically speaking. Furthermore, if you listen to the root of the second dominant chord in the key of the first dominant chord, you will spot that it too is a 'tendency tone', like those we mentioned earlier, in that it tends to fall to the tonic:

Example 87

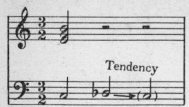

Tendency

Since both dominant chords possess the original tendency tones, it will be realised that the one chord may legitimately be substituted for the other, provided that the melody note allows it:

Example 88

Key C   G11#   C   Db11#   C
        V   I   V[5b sub]   I

This is another device that can add variety when we are thinking out harmonic schemes:

Example 89

Key Eb   Eb6   C7   Fmi7   Bb7   Key Eb   Eb6   Gb7   Fmi7   E7
       I   V of II   II   V   I   V of II [5b sub]   II   V[5b sub]

Note, when comparing the two chords, that the role of the tendency tones is reversed, as are the variable areas:

Example 90

Key C   V   V[5b sub]

The substitution may still be made even if one has to use the tonic melody note, by selecting the substitution major seventh chord:

Example 91

Exercises

(1) Play Example 88 and transpose into all keys.
(2) Compare the role of the tendency tones and variable areas of two dominant chords, a diminished fifth or augmented fourth apart.
(3) Play Example 91 and transpose into all keys.

15 The II/V Combination

In jazz, the seventh chord based on the supertonic (II) degree of the scale is often used in combination with the dominant chord—especially the dominant ninth chord. The two chords have a number of tones in common, and the root of the II chord is a fourth below that of the dominant chord. It thus acts as what might be called the dominant of the dominant:

Example 92

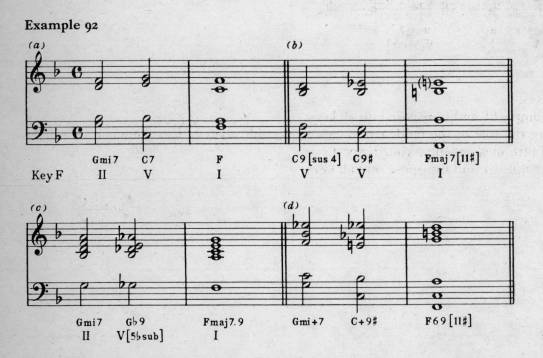

You will observe that here the seventh of the II chord is almost acting as a suspension in the dominant chord; indeed, if you put a dominant bass underneath the II chord it would be complete:

Example 93

The close relationship between the two chords can be effectively exploited in a number of ways, for instance:

Example 94

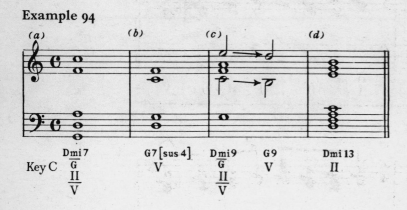

Exercise

Study Example 94 and transpose into all keys, major and minor (using II7(5♭) and V9♭).

16 Pedal Point

In Example 93 we placed a dominant note (V) underneath harmony based on a II chord, thus creating a discord. In this case we 'resolved' it by moving the note to a chordal tone, that is one that belongs to the harmony of the root note. This placing of a sustained note against 'foreign' harmony is called 'pedal point', after its origins in organ music. Any note may be used as a pedal point, but those predominantly found in jazz are the dominant (V) and the tonic (I) notes. The reason probably lies in their function as tonal degrees, i.e. their maintenance of the tonality throughout any 'foreign' harmony. The two notes may be used either singly or in conjunction (in which case they are called a 'double pedal'):

Example 95

In Example 95 the harmony is purely diatonic, but the 'anchoring' effect of the pedal notes is such that the movement of the harmony may be completely arbitrary, following the whims of the melody.

Chromatic harmony may also be used, once again in an arbitrary fashion. Parallel chromatic harmony, in particular, is often combined with pedal point, producing some exciting suspensions which may, or may not, be resolved; here are a few examples:

Parallel major triads

Example 96

Parallel major triads over dominant pedal point

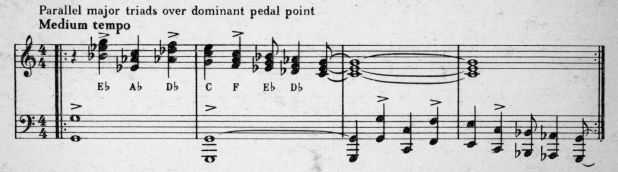

Parallel major seventh chords

Example 97

Parallel major seventh chords over double pedal point

Parallel augmented triads

Example 98

Parallel augmented triads over tonic pedal point

Parallel diminished seventh chords

Example 99

Parallel diminished seventh chords over tonic pedal point

Slowly

Parallel augmented ninth chords

Example 100

Parallel augmented ninth chords over dominant pedal point

Medium tempo

Parallel fourth chords

Example 101

Parallel fourth chords over double pedal point
Fast

As all these resources may be intermingled, the possibilities are virtually limitless. Experiment for yourself. It is best not to think harmonically all the time; try combining skeins of free melody with pedal point, thus creating texture.

Example 102

Counterpoint over tonic pedal point
Slow

The pedal note is not restricted to the lower part; it may also be placed in the middle of harmony (although this presents obvious difficulties when playing the piano). It may also appear above the harmony, when it is called 'inverted pedal point'. Experiment with the preceding examples for these effects.

So far in this chapter we have used pedal point in a very simple way—mostly in the form of sustained notes against harmony. The pedal note can, however, be decorated in many ways, of which the following are among the more obvious:

Example 103

The overall effect of pedal point is to create a static period in music, during which the tension builds up: release is finally attained through resolution, giving the music a new impetus.

Exercises

(1) Study Examples 96, 97, 98, 99, 100, 101 and 102, and experiment in various keys using tonic, dominant or double pedal point.
(2) Play simple right-hand chords and experiment, decorating the pedal note or notes. Maintain a regular rhythm.
(3) Try to incorporate a pedal point into a tune that you already play.

17 The Diminished Scale and Its Ramifications

A diminished scale consists of notes that are alternately a tone and a semitone apart:

Example 104

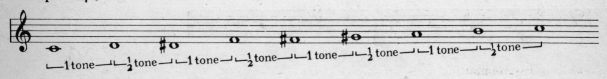

This means in effect that there are only three diminished scales, as each one repeats after being transposed a minor third interval:

Example 105

The basic chord of the diminished scale is the diminished triad, of which there are two, interlocked, in each scale:

Example 106

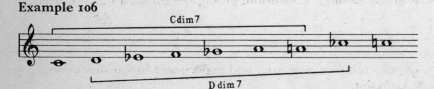

If we superimpose one of these chords on the other and place a root at the distance of a major third underneath the lower chord, thus turning it into a flattened ninth chord, we have a complex dominant chord containing many dissonant intervals:

Example 107

Root — Ab 9b, 11♯, 13, 9♯

Hence, when improvising upon a dominant root, we can make use of this scale:

Example 108

Furthermore, if we study the notes of the scale again, we shall notice that we have fragments from two scales suggesting two dominant chords a diminished fifth apart:[1]

Example 109

Key F   V   V[5b sub]

[1] See Chapter 14.

Although the two interlocked diminished chords are seldom used *in toto*, elements of the combination are often used to add piquancy to the normal diminished sound—sometimes a single note, sometimes two or more notes:

Example 110

Exercises

(1) Play Example 107 and transpose chromatically into all keys. Consider the scale to be used with each dominant chord.

(2) Play a simple dominant seventh in the left hand and improvise over it, using the appropriate diminished scale.

(3) Play a number of diminished chords, altering first one, then two and then three voices to include the related diminished chord (one tone above).

(4) Use these altered diminished chords in the exercises at the end of Chapter 11.

18 The Whole Tone Scale

The whole tone scale is another grouping of tones on which we can improvise, the basic chord here being the augmented triad:

Example 111

Since the scale is symmetrical and the tones two semitones apart, there are only two whole tone scales:

Example 112

The scale can be utilised whenever the augmented triad occurs. This is either as a result of voice leading:

Example 113

or, more statically, as a dominant chord:

Example 114

Key G   Vd of V   Vb   I
         A13   D+9   Gmaj7

By adding notes of the scale to the triad we can construct more dissonant members of the dominant family:

Example 115

Exercises

(1) Play the two whole tone scales.
(2) Identify the augmented triads associated with each scale.
(3) Identify the dominant augmented seventh chords associated with each scale.
(4) Play the dominant augmented seventh chords in all keys with the left hand and improvise on them, using the appropriate whole tone scale.
(5) Play a number of perfect and imperfect cadences in various keys, using the dominant augmented seventh and whole scale to improvise over them.
(6) Transpose Example 113 into the following major keys and improvise over: G, C, F, B♭, E♭, A♭, D♭, etc.

19 The Fourth

The interval of the perfect fourth seems to have been, as it were, a problem child of European music for centuries, and students still find its role ambiguous. Since it is an inversion of the perfect fifth, one would expect it to fall into the same category (that of perfect consonances), but this is not wholly so. The ambiguity seems to lie with the reasons underlying the naming of consonant intervals. Some intervals seem to have been named consonant for the obvious reason that they sound pure (octave and fifth), and on these grounds the fourth is included. But another characteristic of consonant intervals seems to be that they give an impression of finality, and this the fourth does not do. You can test this by playing the following example:

Example 116

Key C G7 C/G C
       V   Ic   I

Note the 'cliff-hanging' effect that results from placing the fifth of the chord in the bass, and how it is alleviated by playing the root at the end.

The fourth interval fell from favour as an exposed harmonic element during the 'reign' of the major/minor system, although it had been extensively used in earlier music. It has now been reinstated, however, and has found particular popularity with jazz musicians during the last few years.

As a harmonic device, chords may be constructed of fourths (instead of thirds) super-imposed on one another:

Example 117

We can best discover their role by first relating them to the major/minor system. The chords in Example 118, based on the I, IV and V notes, are not, of course, true fourth chords, since they have a third as their lowest interval; but I have included them because of their frequent use in major/minor music. They are in fact a particular voicing of a 6/9 chord.

Example 118

The other fourth chords may replace the minor seventh chords which occur on the II, III, VI and VII degrees of the major scale. As we shall see when we come to consider the modern modal system in the next chapter, this use is particularly important.

Example 119

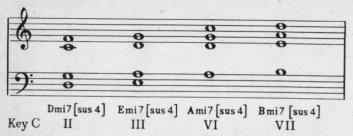

Dmi7 [sus 4]   Emi7 [sus 4]   Ami7 [sus 4]   Bmi7 [sus 4]

Key C   II   III   VI   VII

Exercises

(1) Study Example 118 and transpose into all keys.

(2) Study Example 119 and transpose into all keys.

(3) Substitute fourth chords, where appropriate, in the following sequences and transpose into all keys:

    (a) I, II, V, I.

    (b) I, VI, II, V, I (note the similarities between fourth chords on VI and II).

(4) Play melodic fragments using fourth intervals over I, II, III and VI chords.

(5) Improvise over sequences using original chords but fourth intervals, e.g. C, Ami7, Dmi7, G7. Transpose into other keys.

20   Jazz and the Modal System

We speak of the major and minor 'modes' in tonal music. These are descendants of the original modes, which were used as a basis of musical organisation from the time of the Ancient Greeks until approximately the end of the seventeenth century. At that time they were superseded as the basis of European music by the major/minor system, which in fact developed from the modal system. The trend away from tonal music at the end of the nineteenth century re-established the modes as a useful tool, and their revival has continued to this day. Modern folk-song composers have used them, as did their predecessors; so too have modern classical composers, advanced 'pop' composers and jazz musicians.

Jazz musicians first adopted the modal system as a reaction against the rigid chromatic harmonies of the be-bop era, which had been so thoroughly exploited by its principal exponents, particularly Dizzy Gillespie and Charlie Parker.

Two points must be stressed before we discuss the modern modal system. First, the original modal system was evolved as a means of obtaining different musical colourings from the diatonic scale. At that time the chromatic scale had not yet been discovered, of course; nor had 'mean temperament', i.e. the tuning that permits us to play in different keys. Second, the music was predominantly contrapuntal, in that it consisted of the combination of skeins of melody. The revived modal system is, of course, played on chromatic instruments, and so we can speak of a mode being in a particular key; likewise, jazz musicians are so used to thinking harmonically that they use what might be called a modal harmonic system, a conception that did not exist in the original. Since we are talking about the revived modal system, I intend to discuss it as if it were discovered *after* the major/minor system; and I shall therefore refer to keys and tonalities, although strict musical theory does not admit them in the modal system. The modes, then, may be looked upon as the equivalent of the major scale but with notes other than the tonic used as the key centre. Each mode is called by a Greek name, as follows:

Example 120

(a) Ionian Mode

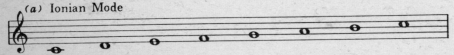

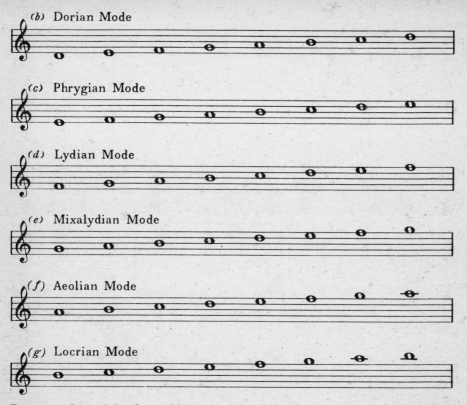

(b) Dorian Mode

(c) Phrygian Mode

(d) Lydian Mode

(e) Mixalydian Mode

(f) Aeolian Mode

(g) Locrian Mode

Because the original music was predominantly vocal the modes had strict ranges, but as we are now talking in instrumental terms we may assume that they extend to the limits of the register.

The first pitfall one comes across when trying to improvise modally is that, having worked with and spent most of one's life listening to tonal music, the absence of tendency tones (which, as we have seen, pull one back to a key) sometimes leads to ambiguity. Furthermore, the tendency tones that we *do* hear often pull us in the wrong direction aurally. This also happens in performances of the original music, but in my view this is a matter more for enjoyment than for regret. If you do wish to establish the 'modal centre' more positively, you can use the device of single or double pedal point; this may be advisable in early experiments.

Example 121

Key C Mixalydian Mode on G

Key C   Dorian Mode on D

Harmonically speaking, the I chord in the mode is the chord that is based on its 'final', that is the modal equivalent of the tonic note. For example, the I chord of the Dorian mode in C would be the chord of D minor, D minor seventh, D minor ninth or D minor eleventh, and so on:

Example 122

Dmi 7   Dmi 9   Dmi 11   Dmi 13

Having established this, we might ask: 'If this is the mode's I chord, what are the chords on the other degrees of the mode?' Theoretically, if we change the bass note we have changed the mode; but in practice it is the frequency and position of the I chord that gives a general 'modal centre'. In any case, it is the musical result of the organisation that is important, rather than the placing of labels.

Modal harmony is often expanded to include diatonic harmony and free modulation, so giving even greater scope. Study some of the compositions in Chapter 22, Section 3, and note the freedom with which modes are treated.

Example 123

Some modes are used more than others. The Ionian mode is seldom thought of as such, since it coincides with our major scale. The Locrian is also seldom used, because of the difficulties of its basic triad, which is diminished. The Dorian, Phrygian, Lydian, Mixalydian and Aeolian modes are all used. Notice the difference between those modes having a basic minor chord (I, III and VI) and those having a major (IV and V).

We noted in Chapter 19 that minor seventh chords may be replaced by chords constructed from perfect fourths. As a result, we often utilise these chords in modal sequences where we might otherwise use minor sevenths. The fourth structure is also used melodically in this example:

Example 124

Key C   Phrygian Mode

We have discussed modal relationships in the key of C only; but the need to be familiar with them in all keys must be stressed, since the static nature of modal harmony often calls for modulation to achieve variety.

The usual method of indicating the scale to be used is to give the 'final' and the mode. Here are some examples of different modes based on the same root:

Example 125

C Dorian   C Phrygian

C Lydian   C Mixalydian

C Aeolian

The scale is usually written in open key (i.e. with accidentals written in), but a key signature is used here as an *aide-memoire*. We might mention here that the use of modes in jazz has led not so much to the adoption of a new (old!) system merely to replace or augment the major/minor system as to a generally freer attitude towards the way in which jazz music is organised; to the use of *other* scales on possibly familiar harmonies; and to a rethinking of the roles to which these vertical combinations of sound have previously adhered rather rigidly.[1]

Exercises

(1) When you have become familiar with the various modes and their basic triads, play a double pedal point with the left hand and extemporise over with the right hand.
(2) Using double pedal point again, improvise in the mode and incorporate free triads in the right hand, as if over a normal double pedal point (i.e. in a key).
(3) Try modes based on other keys.

[1] See Chapter 22, Section 3.

21   The Practical Side

The form of jazz consists predominantly of melody and accompaniment, and these two functions are usually given to the right and left hands respectively. In the early stages the roles will be quite separate, but as you become more adept you will find that they will tend to interchange and intermingle. Sometimes the melody may be played in the bass, while decorative arpeggi or chords may be played by the right hand; or 'spare' fingers in the right hand may accompany a right-hand melody. However, the beginner will need to concentrate so much on other factors, such as accurate rhythm and independent melody, that it is best to start simply, with the left hand playing the accompaniment and the right hand the melody. The following exercises are intended to give practice in inventing phrases in the right hand over a given left-hand bass. The left-hand harmonies are rhythmically simple and easy to finger, and consist of familiar sequences that should be useful also. The roots that have been omitted may be added later, after the exercises have been mastered.

Example 126

(d)

Key F   I   Dim7 link   II   V
F   F#°   Gmi7   C7

Repeat ad lib.

(e)

Key Bb   Vc of V   V   Ic   IV
C7   F7   Bb6   Gmi7

Repeat ad lib.

The exercises in the next group are intended to give early practice in 'stride' left-hand playing: they should be played slowly at first in order to obtain accuracy.

Example 127

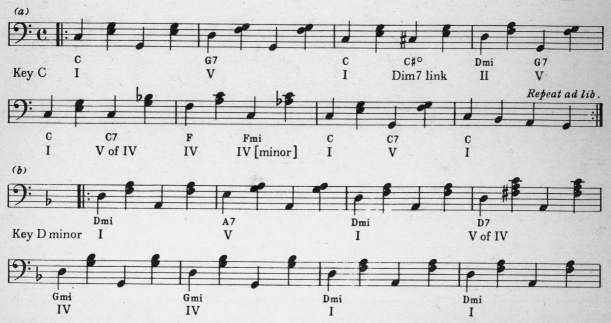

(a)

Key C   I   V   I   Dim7 link   II   V
C   G7   C   C#°   Dmi   G7

I   V of IV   IV   IV [minor]   I   V   I
C   C7   F   Fmi   C   C7   C

Repeat ad lib.

(b)

Key D minor   I   V   I   V of IV
Dmi   A7   Dmi   D7

IV   IV   I   I
Gmi   Gmi   Dmi   Dmi

Superimpose an improvisation when moderate accuracy has been achieved.

Later developments in jazz brought about both rhythmic and harmonic complexities. The use of more complex rhythms for chordal accompaniment to soloists is called 'comping' (short for 'accompanying'). Here are some examples:

Example 128

(a) **Medium tempo**

(b) **Medium slow tempo**

Key D mi.   Dmi   F7/C   Bb13   A+9b   Dmi7♮,9   F13/C   Bb7   A+7   G13 or Dmi69 [add G]
             I   Vb of VI   VI   V   I   Vb of VI   VI   V   I

(c)

Scale C Aeolian   Cmi7   Cmi7   Cmi7   F7/C

Fast

Fmi7   Fmi7   Cmi7   F7/C

Key C minor   Ab7   G+9   Scale C Aeolian
               VI   V

As we saw earlier, certain notes in a chord may be omitted or revoiced in order to make easier execution possible with the left hand. Here are some more examples of this:

Example 129

Since the II and V chords are used in combination so often, you will find the following chromatic exercises for the left hand (in which you should use the minimum of finger movement) of assistance:

Example 130

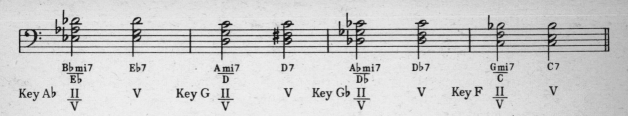

Some sequences give a moving inner part that can act as a counter-melody:

Example 131

May I reiterate here that a single strand of melody carries both rhythmic and harmonic significance, and that *over*-harmonisation is a common fault among budding jazz pianists.

I have attempted to give exercises that will be accessible to different sizes of hand: it is worth mentioning, however, that by attempting to play larger intervals the skin that limits the finger span may be stretched and the span thus increased slightly.

The technique of playing jazz, whatever the instrument, is an integral part of the music. You will find that the two interact, in that you will play phrases that lie under the fingers just as the fingers will attempt to play the phrases you compose in your mind. In written music, pieces are practised to improve technique; similarly, in jazz, pieces tend to become fixed in the mind and practised although they may not be written down. As you progress, the techniques and texture of the music will progress simultaneously; better technique will bring forth more complex phrases that will, in turn, improve the technique. This might not be what is termed 'legitimate' technique (although what that is, is a moot point); nevertheless, if you achieve the result you want with the minimum of effort, it is the right technique for the purpose. Every jazz musician uses a different technique, since some prefer 'singable' phrases to angular phrases, and vice versa; some prefer pure-sounding harmony to exotic sounds, and vice versa. Therefore you have to take selection and rejection decisions the whole time, in order to arrive at a cohesive end product. This is style! But there is one other factor that affects style, and that is physique. Factors such as dexterity, size of hand, memory, intelligence and musical talent all act together to create music, but since there is little that one can do about these factors it is best to ignore them. Concentrate on improving yourself and enjoy it, no matter at what level of ability. This applies just as much to those with advantages as to those who consider themselves handicapped; for the lazy 'natural' jazz musician is a familiar figure also.

22 Some Sequences

The purpose of this final chapter is to provide some material on which to improvise. It is divided into three sections: the first consists of some variations upon the blues; the second, of some standard-type sequences; the third, of contributions by some of the finest composers of jazz at the present time, to whom I would like to express my sincere appreciation.

In the first and second sections I have sketched the harmonic outline in simple, easily playable notation. This is intended merely as an aural guide and may be utilised or discarded when improvising. It is, of course, important that the exercises be played in strict rhythm.

It is, of course, impossible to give every alternative that exists in music in *any* book, let alone in one as brief as this. *Jazz Piano* does not attempt to do this; it has been written merely as a 'launching pad' for those who enjoy creating jazz music at the keyboard. It has been necessary to have recourse to systems in the book; but systems impose their own limitations on music and can reduce it to a succession of mere formulae (as has happened at certain periods in both European music and jazz). It is therefore necessary to stress again that a musician should have the courage of his or her convictions, and trust to those subconscious processes that have been responsible for the creation of great music in all spheres, rather than merely to remain within the confines of rules and formulae.

1 The blues

Example 132

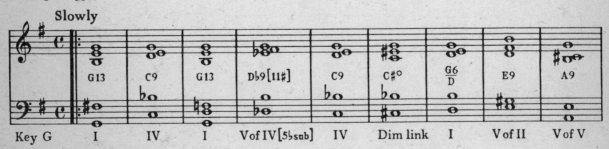

Example 134

Example 135

Example 136

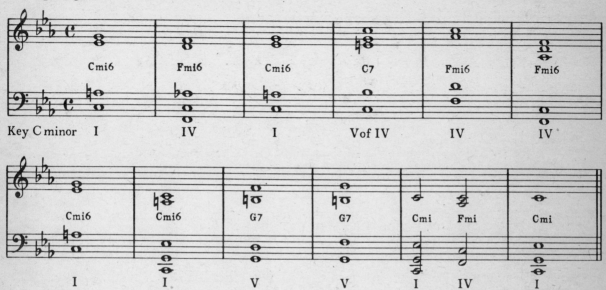

Key C minor   I   IV   I   V of IV   IV   IV

Cmi6   Fmi6   Cmi6   C7   Fmi6   Fmi6

Cmi6   Cmi6   G7   G7   Cmi   Fmi   Cmi

I   I   V   V   I   IV   I

Example 137

Fmi   Ab7/Eb   Db9[11#]   C9b   Fmi   Bbmi   Cmi7   F9

Key F minor   I   Vc of VI   VI   V   I   IV   II of IV   IV

Bbmi   Bbmi6   Bbmi[7♮]   Bbmi6   Fmi   Fmi+   Fmi6   Fmi7   Db9   Db9[11#]

IV   IV   I   I   VI   VI

Example 138

2 Standard-type sequences

Example 139   *Lazy River*   H. Carmichael & S. Arodin

Example 140

Rockin' Chair

H. Carmichael

Example 141   *I'm Getting Sentimental Over You*   George Bassman &
                                                                                     Ned Washington

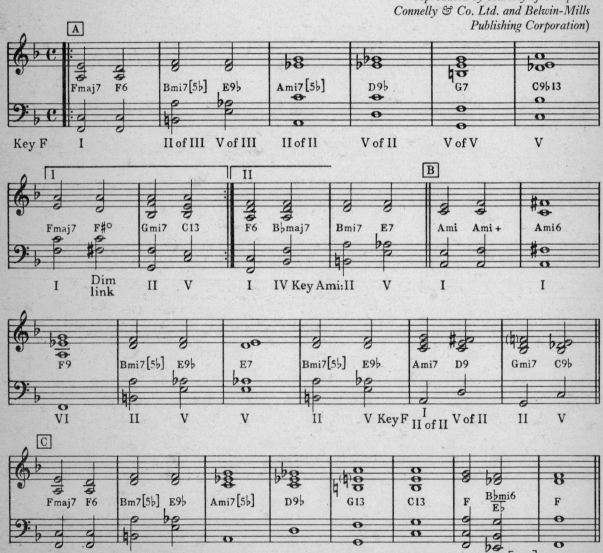

Example 142   *You Can Depend On Me*   C. Carpenter, L. Dunlap & E. Hines

Example 143   *Ain't Misbehavin'*   Fats Waller

Example 144

Medium tempo

Example 145

B°7 | F | Eb7 | D7 | G7 | C7 | F

Dim link | I | V of VI [5b sub] | V of II | V of V | V | I

Example 146

Medium slow

F7 | Bb7 | Eb6 | Cmi7 | F7 | Bb7 | Eb

Key Eb | V of V | V | I | VI | V of V | V | I

Eb7 | D7 | Db7 | C7 | F7 | Bb7 | Eb

I | V of III | V of VI [5b sub] | V of II | V of V | V | I

Example 147

Medium fast

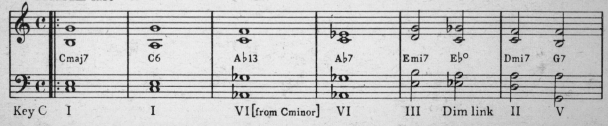

Cmaj7 | C6 | Ab13 | Ab7 | Emi7 | Eb° | Dmi7 | G7

Key C | I | I | VI [from C minor] | VI | III | Dim link | II | V

Example 148

Medium fast tempo

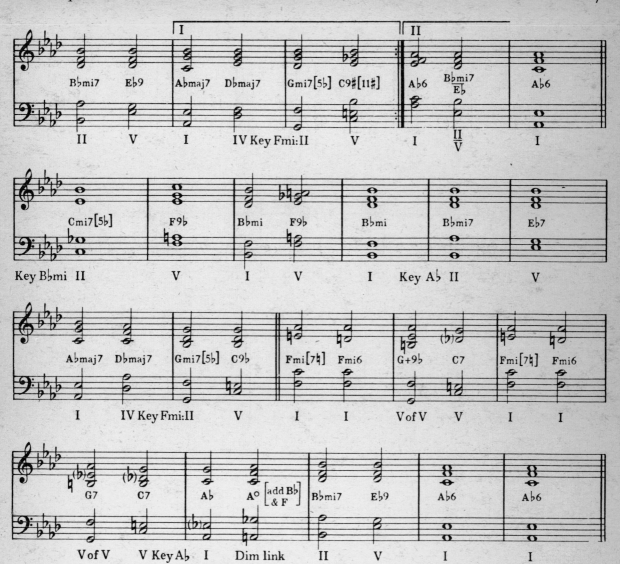

Example 149

Example 150

3 Modern jazz compositions

Example 151   *Amoroso Only More So*   Stan Tracy

Example 152   *Rainbow At The Five Mile Road*   Stan Tracy

Example 153

Love Now, Weep Later

Stan Tracy

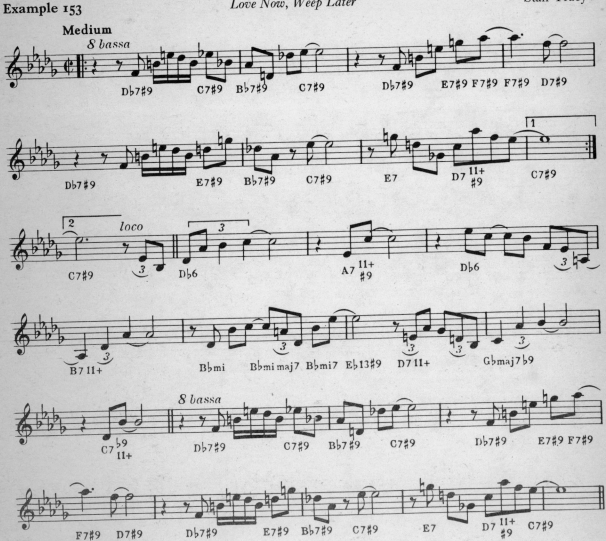

Example 154   *Tucky-Tah, Tucky-Tah-Tah*   Stan Tracy

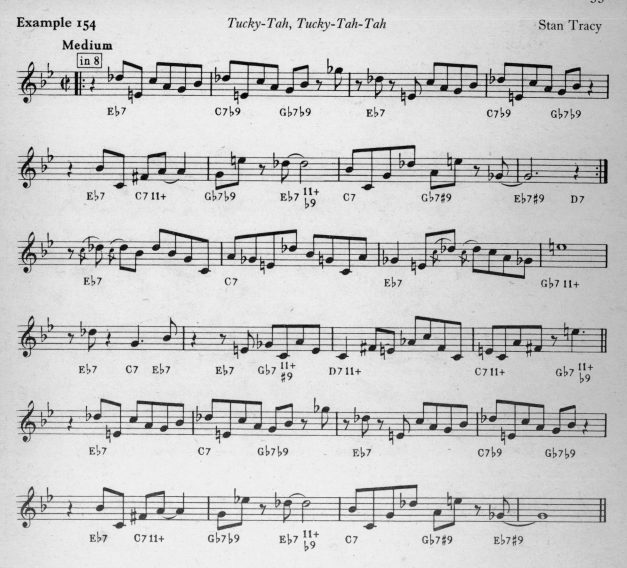

Example 155   *Panto Panta*   Stan Tracy

Example 156   *Sound of Seventeen*   Harry South
(*Published by Stanza Music*)

Example 157   *The Scandinavian*   Harry South
(*Published by Stanza Music*)

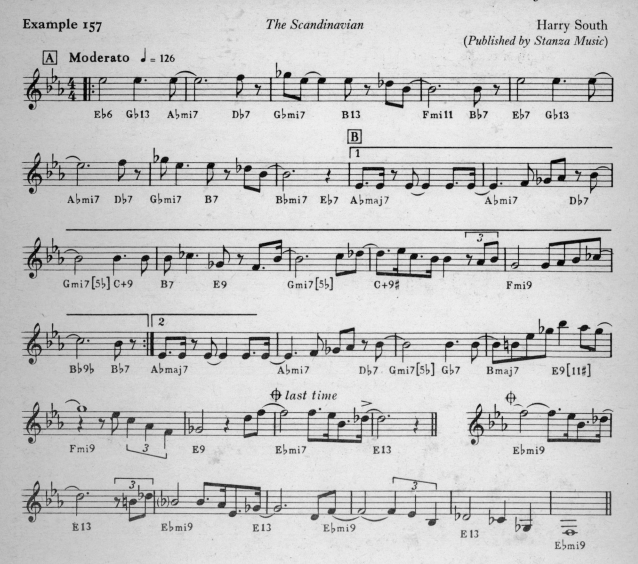

Example 158 *North of the Soho Border* Harry South
(*Published by Stanza Music*)

Example 159 *The Sweet Yakity Waltz* Ken Wheeler

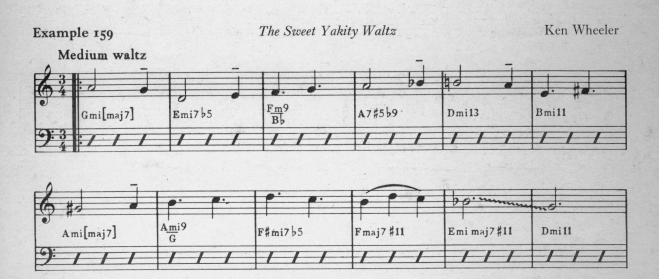

Example 160   *Altisadora*   Ken Wheeler

Medium Bossa Nova

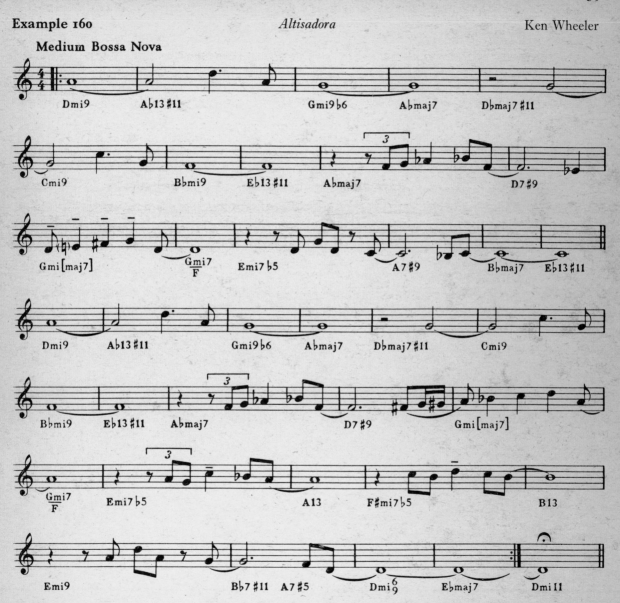

Example 161 *Don No More* Ken Wheeler

Example 162 *E.K.I. (Everybody Knows It)* Ken Wheeler

Example 163   *Feelings and Things*   Michael Gibbs
          (Published by Grayfriar Music)

Example 164   *Blue Comedy*   Michael Gibbs
(*Published by Burrows Music*)

Example 165 *Fly Time Fly (Sigh)* Michael Gibbs
(*Published by M.J.Q. Music*)

Example 166   *Nonsequence*   Michael Gibbs

Example 167   *And on the Third Day*   Michael Gibbs
(*Published by Grayfriar Music*)

Slow ♩ = 60 (Rock feeling)

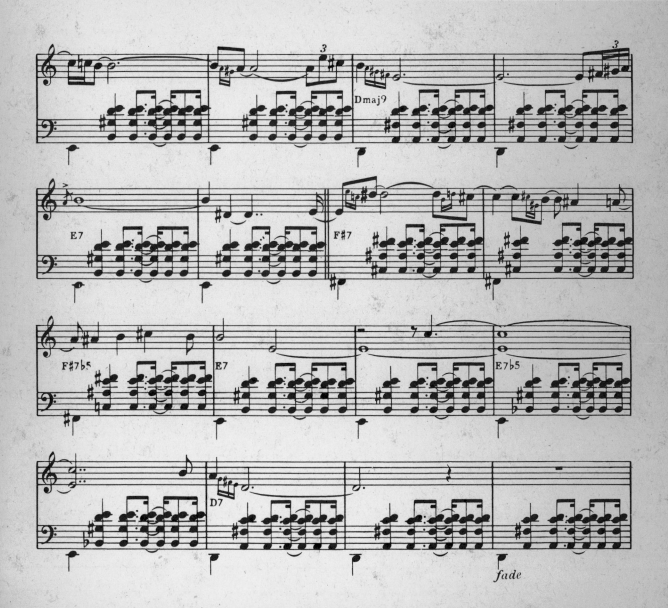

Example 168   *Sweet Rain*   Michael Gibbs
(Published by On Stage Publishing Co.)

(Rhythm: Gently imply double time _ _ _ _ _ _ _ _ _ _ _ _ _ _ _)

Example 169   *The Imaginary Mirror*   John Warren
(Published by Stanza Music)

Open key

Moderately fast

Example 170   *Picture-Tree*   John Warren
                                                         (*Published by Indian Brandee*)

Open key
Moderate

Example 171

Skating

John Warren
(Published by Indian Brandee)

Open key
Moderate

Example 172   *Time Running Backwards*   John Warren
                                                           (*Published by P.R.S.*)

Open key
Slow – rubato

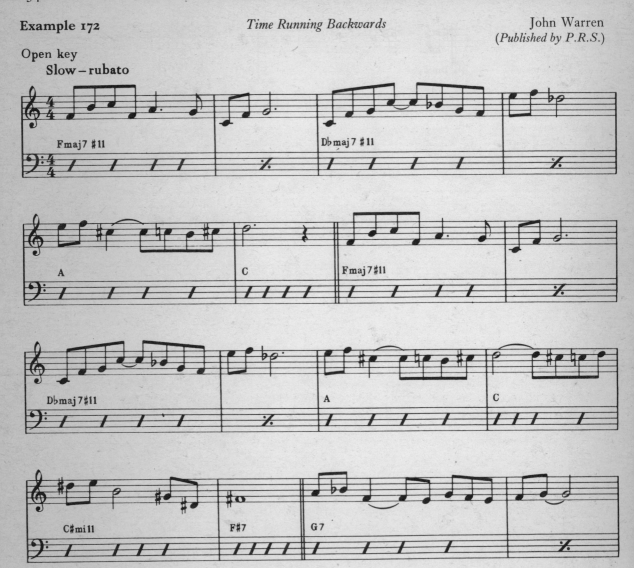

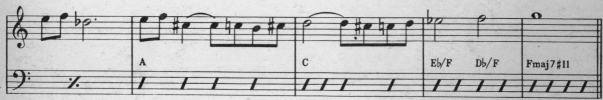

Example 173   *Changes For Blowing*   John Warren

Moderately fast

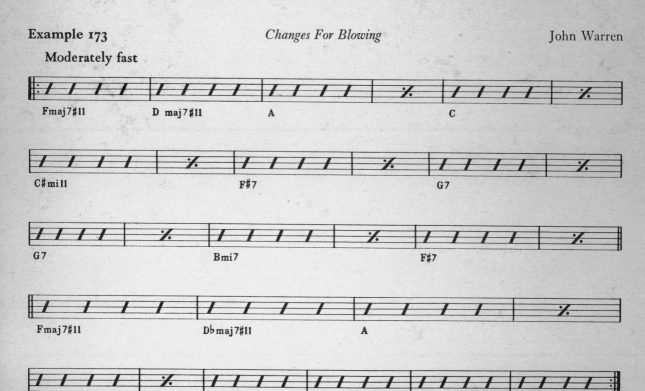

Example 174   *Pastorale*   Pat Smythe
(*Published by M.S.S.*)

ad lib. fade on these 2 chords

Example 175   *Regrets*   Pat Smythe
(Published by Essex Music)

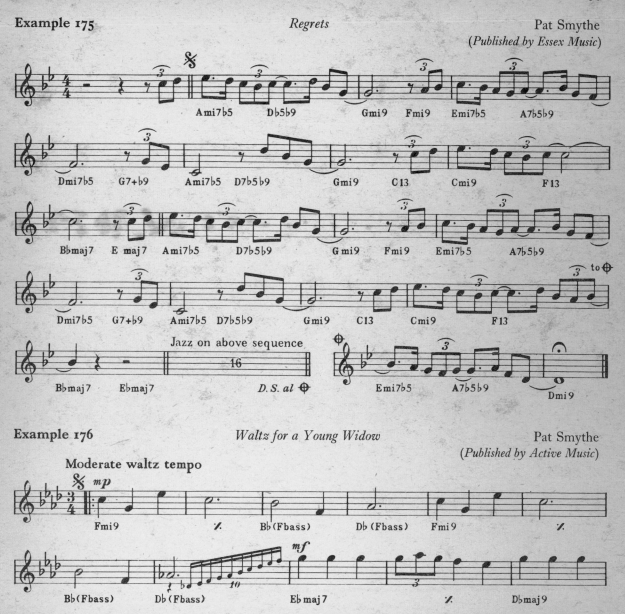

Example 176   *Waltz for a Young Widow*   Pat Smythe
(Published by Active Music)

Example 177   *Joy*   Pat Smythe
                                                                      (*Published by Airborne Music*)

Example 178   *Glancing Backwards*   John Surman

Example 179   *Throwley Forstal*   John Surman

Example 180   *Tryst*   Mike Pyne

Example 181

Carol's Carrot,

Mike Pyne

Start improvisation on bar 3 of the theme

Bibliography

I have found the following books useful, but I believe that, since jazz is only one branch of a great art, finding out anything anywhere about music has some bearing upon one's ability as a jazz musician.

Elementary

Introducing Music	Otto Karolyi	Pelican
The ABC of Music	Imogen Holst	O.U.P.
The Piano	King Palmer	Teach Yourself Books

Intermediate

Harmony	Walter Piston	Norton
Counterpoint	Walter Piston	Norton
Elementary Training for Musicians	Paul Hindemith	Schott
Twentieth Century Harmony	V. Persichetti	Faber & Faber
Traditional Harmony	Paul Hindemith	Schott
Harmony	Peter Wishart	Hutchinson
The Art of Counterpoint	C. H. Kitson	O.U.P.
Counterpoint	Edmund Rubbra	Hutchinson

Advanced

Contemporary Harmony	Ludmilla Ullela	Macmillan (N.Y.)
A Study of Twentieth Century Harmony (Vol. II)	Mosco Carner	Galliard Ltd.

Piano studies

Studies and Exercises for Piano, Opus 139	Carl Czerny	Galliard Ltd.
Studies for Piano (No. 806a)	J. B. Cramer	Galliard Ltd.
Daily Technical Studies for the Pianoforte (No. 267)	Oscar Berringer	Bosworth & Co. Ltd.

TEACH YOURSELF BOOKS

THE PIANO

C. King Palmer

This book does not claim to teach the reader to become an accomplished pianist, but rather to provide sufficient information and instruction for the beginner to learn to play with confidence and enjoyment.

Both the theory of piano music and the principles of the instrument are explained in the first chapters, on the assumption that some readers will know nothing of either. The book then takes the reader through the technique and practice of piano playing, discussing such problems as fingering and phrasing, and advising the student on how gradually to develop his skill.

A thorough and practical guide to the theory and practice of piano playing, invaluable both to the complete beginner and the student.

ISBN 0 340 056886

Available wherever Teach Yourself Books are sold

TEACH YOURSELF BOOKS

THE GUITAR

Dale Fradd

The Spanish or classical guitar today enjoys tremendous popularity: concert-halls are full, guitar societies flourish everywhere and it is currently the instrument most in demand by school children. But there are still few good guitar teachers, and many people try to teach themselves to play the instrument.

This book offers a complete, step-by-step guide to playing the classical guitar for beginners and those who have perhaps tried unsuccessfully in the past to teach themselves the instrument. It covers everything, from buying the guitar, to tuning it, to reading the music to actually playing it. The classical technique, essential to the successful guitarist, is described in detail with the help of photographs, and many examples of studies and pieces representing the wide variety of classical guitar music are included.

With this book and by practising regularly, anyone can become a guitarist of at least reasonable proficiency.

ISBN 0 340 16197 3

Available wherever Teach Yourself Books are sold